MW01179147

EXCEL 5
FOR WINDOWS™

VISUAL
PocketGuide

by: maranGraphics' Development Group

Excel 5 for Windows™ Visual PocketGuide

Published 1994
Canadian Cataloging in Publication Data
Maran, Ruth, 1970-
    MaranGraphics Microsoft Excel 5 for Windows :
pocket guide

Includes index.
ISBN 0-9695666-5-4

1. Microsoft Excel for Windows (Computer file).
2. Business - Computer programs. 3. Electronic
spreadsheets. I. Title. II. Title: Microsoft
Excel 5 for Windows.

HF5548.4.M523M3 1994   005.369   C94-932367-5

Printed in the United States of America

10   9   8   7   6   5   4   3   2   1

Trademark Acknowledgments

maranGraphics Inc. has attempted to include trademark information for products, services and companies referred to in this guide. Although maranGraphics Inc. has made reasonable efforts in gathering this information, it cannot guarantee its accuracy.

Microsoft, MS, MS-DOS, and XL design (the Microsoft Excel logo) are registered trademarks and AutoSum, Windows, and Windows NT are trademarks of Microsoft Corporation in the United States of America and other countries.

©1994
maranGraphics, Inc.

The animated characters are the
copyright of maranGraphics, Inc.

Credits

Author & Architect:
Ruth Maran

Copy Developer:
Kelleigh Wing

Technical Consultant:
Wendi Blouin Ewbank

Layout Artist:
Christie Van Duin

Designer:
David de Haas

Illustrator:
Dave Ross

Editor:
Judy Maran

Post Production:
Robert Maran

Acknowledgments

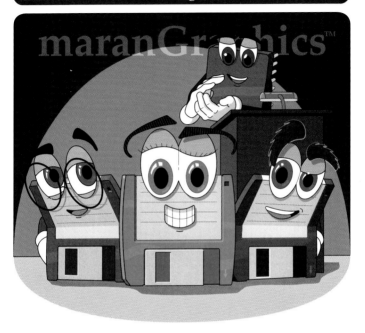

Thanks to Terry Blanchard of Microsoft Canada Inc. for his support and consultation.

Thanks to Wendi B. Ewbank for her dedication and support in ensuring the technical accuracy of this book.

Thanks also to Saverio C. Tropiano for his assistance and expert advice.

Thanks to the dedicated staff of maranGraphics, including David de Haas, Peters Ezers, David Hendricks, Jill Maran, Judy Maran, Maxine Maran, Robert Maran, Dave Ross, Christie Van Duin, Carol Walthers and Kelleigh Wing.

Finally, to Richard Maran who originated the easy-to-use graphic format of this guide. Thank you for your inspiration and guidance.

TABLE OF CONTENTS

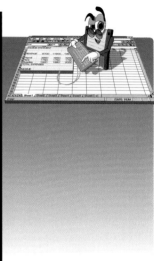

TABLE OF CONTENTS

Using Multiple Workbooks

Charting Data

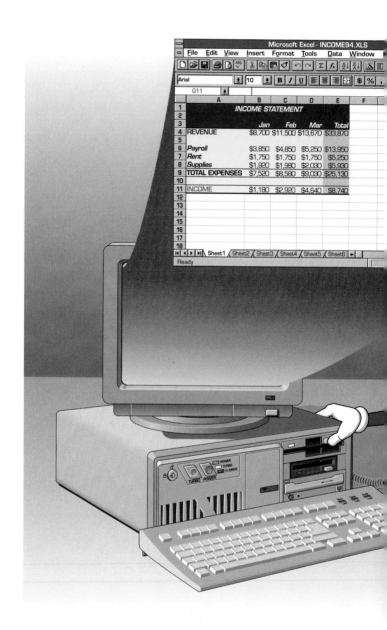

Microsoft®
Excel 5.0 for
Windows™ is a
spreadsheet program
that will save you time
and increase the
accuracy of your
calculations.

INTRODUCTION

This is what you can create with Excel for Windows.

PERSONAL FINANCES

Excel helps you keep track of your mortgage, balance your checkbook, create a personal budget, compare investments and prepare your taxes.

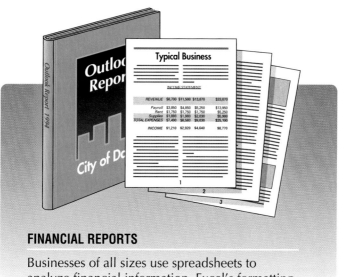

FINANCIAL REPORTS

Businesses of all sizes use spreadsheets to analyze financial information. Excel's formatting and charting features help you present your results in professional looking documents.

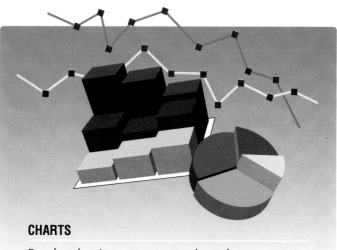

CHARTS

Excel makes it easy to create charts from your spreadsheet data. Charts let you visually illustrate the relationship between different items.

USING THE MOUSE

The mouse is a hand-held device that lets you quickly select commands and perform tasks.

USING THE MOUSE

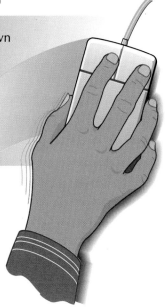

◆ Hold the mouse as shown in the diagram. Use your thumb and two rightmost fingers to guide the mouse while your two remaining fingers press the mouse buttons.

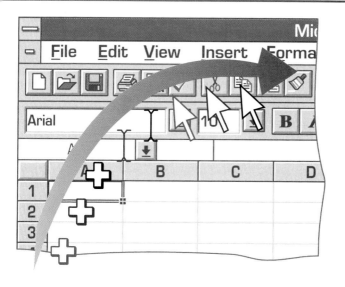

◆ When you move the mouse on your desk,
the mouse pointer (⊹, I or ◌) on your screen
moves in the same direction. The mouse pointer
changes shape depending on its location on
your screen and the action you are performing.

USING THE MOUSE

PARTS OF THE MOUSE

◆ The mouse has a left and right button. You can use these buttons to:

- open menus
- select commands
- choose options

Note: You will use the left button most of the time.

MOUSE TERMS

CLICK

Quickly press and release the left mouse button once.

DOUBLE-CLICK

Quickly press and release the left mouse button twice.

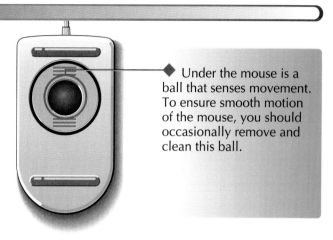

Under the mouse is a ball that senses movement. To ensure smooth motion of the mouse, you should occasionally remove and clean this ball.

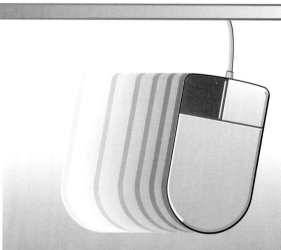

DRAG

When the mouse pointer (✛ , I or ⌖) is over an object on your screen, press and hold down the left mouse button and then move the mouse.

START EXCEL

When you start Excel, a blank worksheet appears. You can enter data into this worksheet.

START EXCEL

C:\> win _

1 To start Excel from MS-DOS, type **win** and then press **Enter**.

10

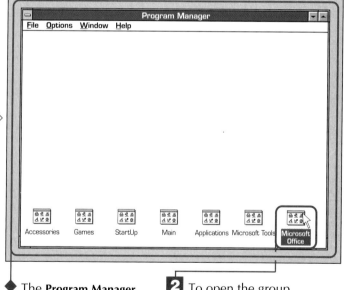

◆ The **Program Manager**
window appears.

2 To open the group
window that contains Excel,
move the mouse ⇧ over the
icon (example: **Microsoft Office**)
and then quickly press the left
button twice.

To continue, refer to the next page.

START EXCEL

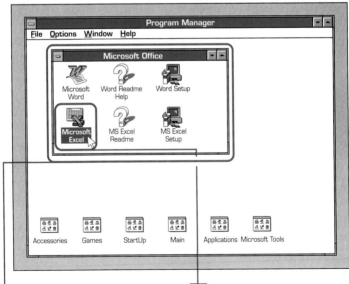

◆ The group window opens.

3 To start the Excel application, move the mouse ⬚ over **Microsoft Excel** and then quickly press the left button twice.

12

The worksheet displayed on your screen is part of a workbook. A workbook is like a three-ring binder that contains several sheets of paper.

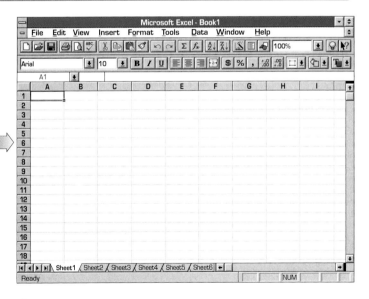

◆ The **Microsoft Excel** window appears, displaying a blank worksheet.

EXCEL BASICS

COLUMNS, ROWS AND CELLS

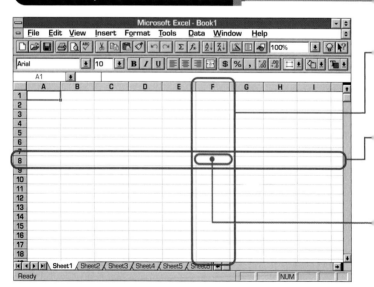

A worksheet consists of columns, rows and cells.

◆ **Column**
A column is a vertical line of boxes. Excel labels the columns in a worksheet (example: **F**).

◆ **Row**
A row is a horizontal line of boxes. Excel numbers the rows in a worksheet (example: **8**).

◆ **Cell**
A cell is the area where a column and row intersect (example: **F8**).

CHANGE THE ACTIVE CELL

CHANGE THE ACTIVE CELL

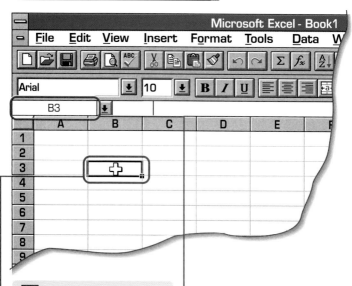

1 To make another cell on your screen the active cell, move the mouse ⊹ over the cell and then press the left button.

◆ The cell now displays a thick border.

◆ A **cell reference** defines the location of each cell. It consists of a column letter followed by a row number (example: **B3**).

◆ The cell reference of the active cell appears at the top of your worksheet.

The active cell displays a thick border. You can only enter data into the active cell.

USING THE KEYBOARD

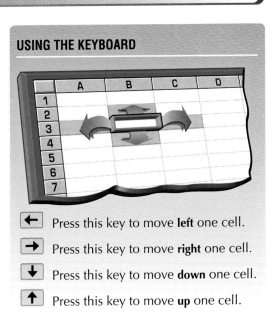

← Press this key to move **left** one cell.

→ Press this key to move **right** one cell.

↓ Press this key to move **down** one cell.

↑ Press this key to move **up** one cell.

ENTER DATA

ENTER DATA

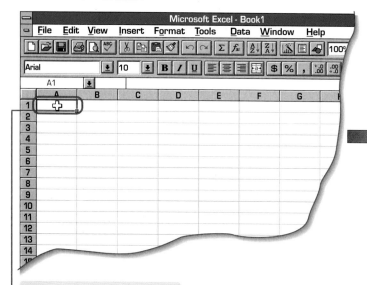

1 Move the mouse ✛ over the cell where you want to enter data (example: **A1**) and then press the left button.

◆ The cell becomes the active cell and displays a thick border.

18

You can use the keyboard to enter data into your worksheet.

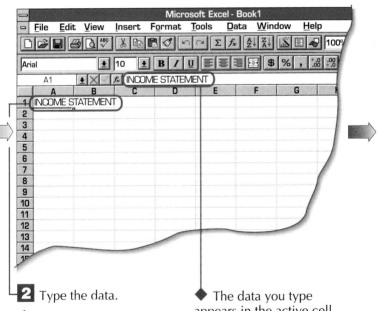

2 Type the data.

◆ If you make a typing mistake, press **+Backspace** on your keyboard to remove the incorrect text and then retype.

◆ The data you type appears in the active cell and in the formula bar.

To continue, refer to the next page.

19

ENTER DATA

Text — Left Align

8700 — Right Align

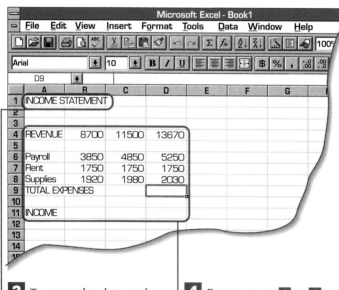

	A	B	C	D	E	F	G
1	INCOME STATEMENT						
2							
3							
4	REVENUE	8700	11500	13670			
5							
6	Payroll	3850	4850	5250			
7	Rent	1750	1750	1750			
8	Supplies	1920	1980	2030			
9	TOTAL EXPENSES						
10							
11	INCOME						
12							
13							
14							

3 To enter the data and move down one cell, press **Enter**.

or

To enter the data and move one cell in any direction, press **→**, **←**, **↓** or **↑**.

4 Repeat steps **1** to **3** starting on page 18, until you finish entering all your data.

When you enter data in a worksheet, Excel automatically left aligns the text and right aligns the numbers.

LONG LABELS

◆ If a label you type is too long to fit in one cell, the text will spill over into neighboring cells if they are empty.

◆ If the neighboring cell contains data, Excel will display as much of the label as the column width will allow.

LONG NUMBERS

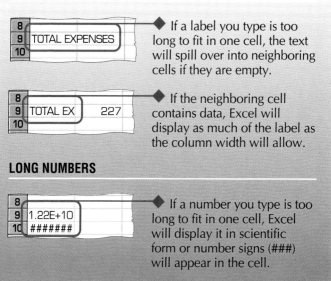

◆ If a number you type is too long to fit in one cell, Excel will display it in scientific form or number signs (###) will appear in the cell.

Note: To display an entire label or number, you must increase the column width. For more information, refer to page 130.

SELECT CELLS

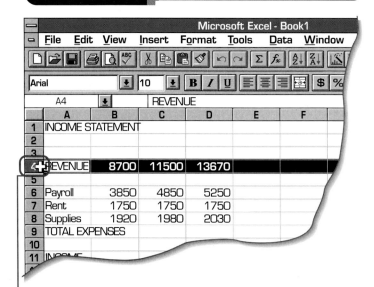

1 Move the mouse ⊹ over the row number you want to select (example: **4**) and then press the left button.

◆ Make sure the mouse looks like ⊹ (not ⊕) before pressing the button.

Note: To cancel a selection, move the mouse ⊹ over any cell in your worksheet and then press the left button.

Before you can use many Excel features, you must first select the cells you want to work with.

SELECT A COLUMN

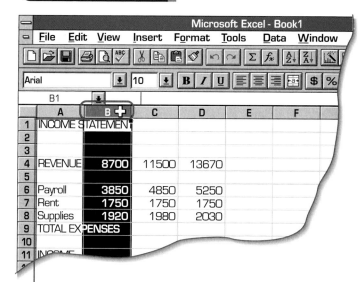

1 Move the mouse ⌐⊦ over the column letter you want to select (example: **B**) and then press the left button.

◆ Make sure the mouse looks like ⌐⊦ (not ↔) before pressing the button.

23

SELECT CELLS

SELECT A GROUP OF CELLS

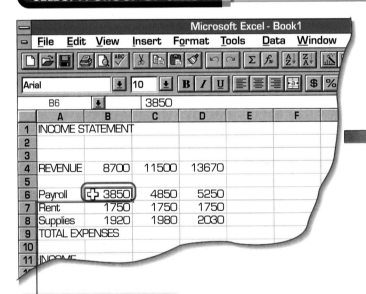

1 Move the mouse 🖑 over the first cell you want to select (example: **B6**) and then press and hold down the left button.

Selected cells appear highlighted on your screen.

SELECT THE ENTIRE WORKSHEET

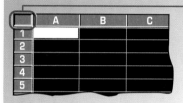

1 Move the mouse ⊹ over the area where the row and column headings intersect and then press the left button.

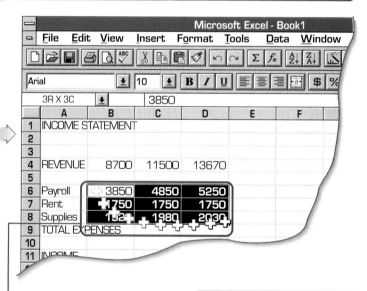

	Microsoft Excel - Book1					
File	Edit	View	Insert	Format	Tools	Data	Window

Arial ± 10 ± **B** *I* <u>U</u> | | | | \$ %

3R X 3C	±		3850			
	A	**B**	**C**	**D**	**E**	**F**
1	INCOME STATEMENT					
2						
3						
4	REVENUE	8700	11500	13670		
5						
6	Payroll	3850	4850	5250		
7	Rent	1750	1750	1750		
8	Supplies	1924	1980	2030		
9	TOTAL EXPENSES					
10						
11	INCOME					

2 Still holding down the button, drag the mouse ⊹ until you highlight all the cells you want to select.

3 Release the button.

SELECT TWO GROUPS OF CELLS

To select another group of cells, press and hold down **Ctrl** while repeating steps **1** to **3**.

25

USING AUTOFILL

USING AUTOFILL TO COMPLETE A SERIES

COMPLETE A SERIES OF LABELS

Monday	Tuesday	Wednesday	Thursday
Product 1	Product 2	Product 3	Product 4
Q1	Q2	Q3	Q4

◆ Excel completes a series of labels based on the label in the first cell.

COMPLETE A SERIES OF NUMBERS

1993	1994	1995	1996
1	2	3	4
5	10	15	20

◆ Excel completes a series of numbers based on the numbers in the first two cells. These numbers tell Excel how much to add to each number to complete the series.

You can save time by using the AutoFill feature to complete a series of labels or numbers in your worksheet.

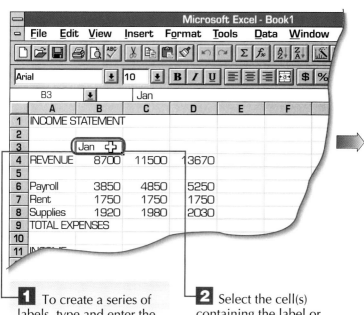

1 To create a series of labels, type and enter the first label in the series (example: **Jan**).

◆ To create a series of numbers, type and enter the first two numbers in the series.

2 Select the cell(s) containing the label or numbers you entered.

Note: To select cells, refer to pages 22 to 25.

To continue, refer to the next page.

USING AUTOFILL

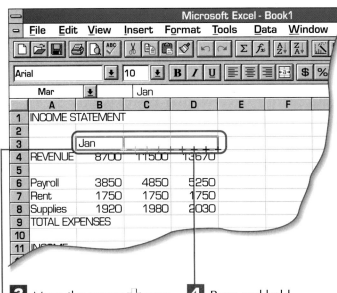

3 Move the mouse ⫰ over the bottom right corner of the selected cell(s) and ⫰ changes to +.

4 Press and hold down the left button as you drag the mouse + over the cells you want to include in the series.

The AutoFill feature is useful when adding headings or a series of numbers to your worksheet.

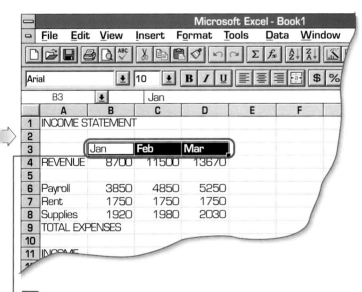

5 Release the button and the cells display the series.

Note: You can also use the AutoFill feature to fill data in columns.

SELECT COMMANDS

You can open a menu to display a list of related commands. You can then select the command you want to use.

USING THE MOUSE

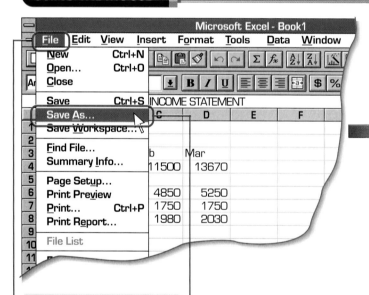

1 To open a menu, move the mouse ⟍ over the menu name (example: **File**) and then press the left button.

◆ A menu appears, displaying a list of related commands.

Note: To close a menu, move the mouse ⟍ anywhere over your worksheet and then press the left button.

2 To select a command, move the mouse ⟍ over the command name (example: **Save As**) and then press the left button.

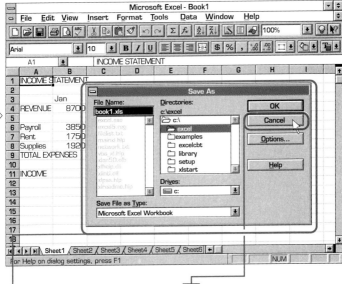

◆ A dialog box appears if Excel requires more information to carry out the command.

3 To close a dialog box, move the mouse ⏳ over **Cancel** and then press the left button.

SELECT COMMANDS

You can use the keyboard to select a command.

USING THE KEYBOARD

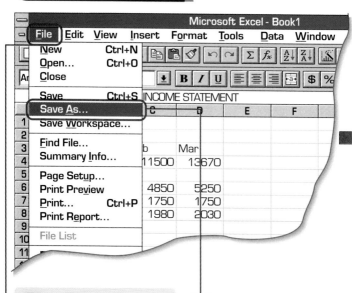

1 To open a menu, press Alt followed by the underlined letter in the menu name (example: F for **File**).

Note: To close a menu, press Alt.

2 To select a command, press the underlined letter in the command name (example: A for **Save As**).

File

New	Ctrl+N
O**pen**...	Ctrl+O
Close	
Save	Ctrl+S
Save **As**...	
Save **Workspace**...	
Find File...	
Summary **Info**...	
Page Set**up**...	
Print Prev...	

◆ If key names are separated by a plus sign (+), press and hold down the first key before pressing the second key (example: `Ctrl` + `N`).

◆ Some commands display a keyboard shortcut (example: press `Ctrl` + `N` to select the **New** command).

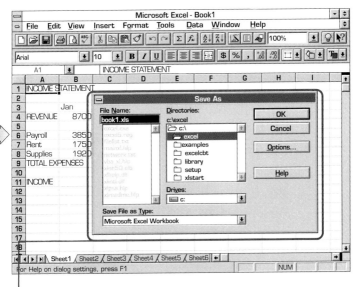

◆ A dialog box appears if Excel requires more information to carry out the command.

3 To close a dialog box, press `Esc` .

THE EXCEL BUTTONS

THE EXCEL BUTTONS

Each button displayed on your screen provides a fast method of selecting a menu command.

For example, you can use 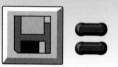 to quickly select the Save command.

File	
<u>N</u>ew	Ctrl+N
<u>O</u>pen...	Ctrl+O
<u>C</u>lose	
<u>S</u>ave	Ctrl+S
Save <u>A</u>s...	
Save <u>W</u>orkspace...	
<u>F</u>ind File...	

You can use the Excel buttons to quickly select the most commonly used commands.

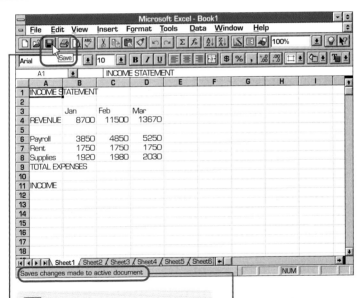

1 To view a description of a button displayed on your screen, move the mouse ↖ over the button of interest (example: 🔲).

◆ After a few seconds, the name of the button appears in a yellow box.

◆ A short description of the button also appears at the bottom of your screen.

35

MOVE THROUGH A WORKSHEET

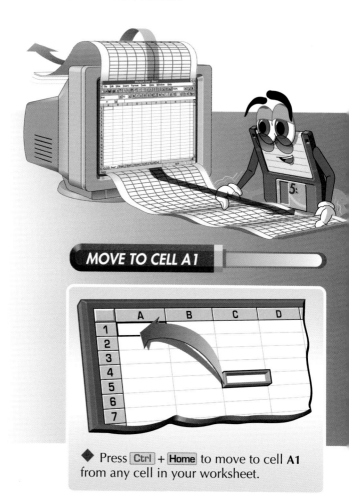

MOVE TO CELL A1

◆ Press **Ctrl** + **Home** to move to cell **A1** from any cell in your worksheet.

If your worksheet contains a lot of data, your computer screen cannot display all of the data at the same time. You must scroll up or down to view other parts of your worksheet.

MOVE ONE SCREEN UP OR DOWN

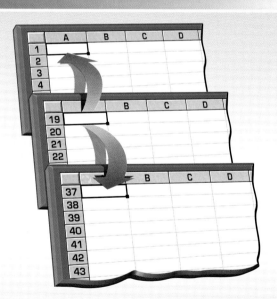

◆ Press **PageDown** to move down one screen.

◆ Press **PageUp** to move up one screen.

◆ Press **Alt** + **PageDown** to move right one screen.

◆ Press **Alt** + **PageUp** to move left one screen.

MOVE THROUGH A WORKSHEET

SCROLL UP OR DOWN

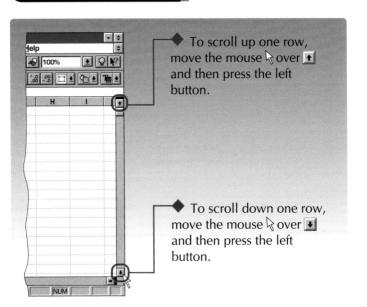

◆ To scroll up one row, move the mouse ⬇ over 🔺 and then press the left button.

◆ To scroll down one row, move the mouse ⬇ over 🔻 and then press the left button.

SCROLL LEFT OR RIGHT

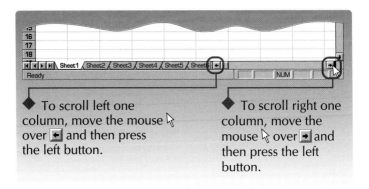

◆ To scroll left one column, move the mouse ⬇ over ◀ and then press the left button.

◆ To scroll right one column, move the mouse ⬇ over ▶ and then press the left button.

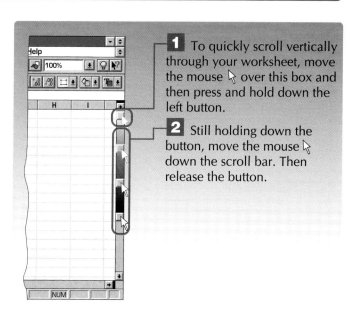

1 To quickly scroll vertically through your worksheet, move the mouse ⟨⟩ over this box and then press and hold down the left button.

2 Still holding down the button, move the mouse ⟨⟩ down the scroll bar. Then release the button.

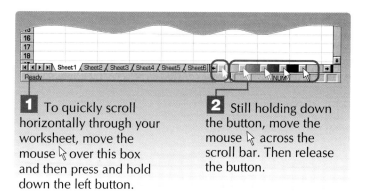

1 To quickly scroll horizontally through your worksheet, move the mouse ⟨⟩ over this box and then press and hold down the left button.

2 Still holding down the button, move the mouse ⟨⟩ across the scroll bar. Then release the button.

GETTING HELP

If you forget how to perform a task, you can use the Help feature to obtain information.

GETTING HELP

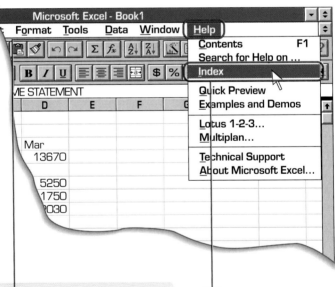

1 To display the Microsoft Excel Help Index, move the mouse ⬡ over **Help** and then press the left button.

2 Move the mouse ⬡ over **Index** and then press the left button.

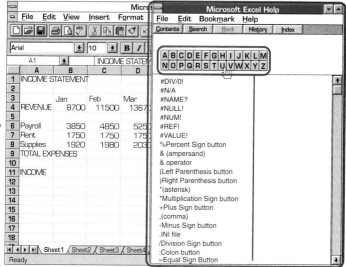

◆ The **Microsoft Excel Help** window appears.

3 Move the mouse 🖑 over the first letter of the topic you want information on (example: **U** for **Underlining**) and then press the left button.

To continue, refer to the next page.

41

GETTING HELP

> The Help feature can save you time by eliminating the need to refer to other sources.

GETTING HELP (CONTINUED)

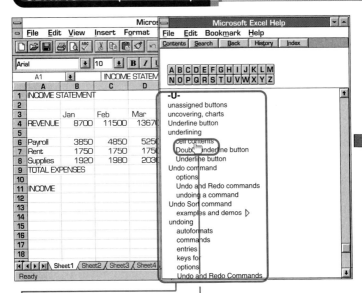

◆ Topics beginning with the letter you selected appear.

◆ To view more topics beginning with the letter, press **PageDown** on your keyboard.

4 Move the mouse over the topic of interest and then press the left button.

THE TIPWIZARD

If Excel knows a better way to accomplish a task you are performing, the TipWizard button will turn from white to yellow.

1 To display the tip, move the mouse ⌖ over 🔲 and then press the left button. The tip appears.

Note: To hide the tip, repeat step 1.

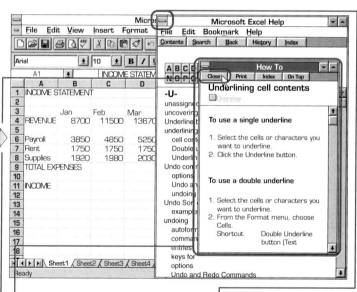

◆ Information on the topic you selected appears.

5 To close the **How To** window, move the mouse ⌖ over **Close** and then press the left button.

6 To close the **Microsoft Excel Help** window, move the mouse ⌖ over ⊟ and then quickly press the left button twice.

DRIVES

Your computer stores programs and data in devices called "drives." Like a filing cabinet, a drive stores information in an organized way.

Most computers have one hard drive and one or two floppy drives to store information.

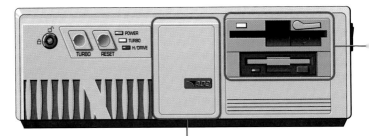

Hard drive (C:)

◆ The hard drive magnetically stores information inside your computer. It is called drive **C**.

*Note: Your computer may be set up to have additional hard drives (example: **drive D**).*

Drive Name

A: ◆ A drive name consists of two parts: the letter and a colon (:). The colon represents the word "drive." For example, **A**: refers to the **A drive.**

Floppy drives (A: and B:)

◆ A floppy drive stores information on removable diskettes (or floppy disks). A diskette operates slower and stores less data than a hard drive.

Diskettes are used to:

- Load new programs.
- Store backup copies of data.
- Transfer data to other computers.

If your computer has only one floppy drive, it is called drive **A**.

If your computer has two floppy drives, the second drive is called drive **B**.

Hard Drive (C:)

The hard drive stores your programs and data. It contains many directories to organize your information.

Files

When you save a workbook, Excel stores it as a file.

Directories

A directory usually contains related information. For example, the **excel** directory contains the Microsoft Excel files.

NAME A WORKBOOK

When you save a workbook for the first time, you must give it a name.

A file name consists of two parts: a name and an extension. You must separate these parts with a period.

INCOME94.XLS

Name

The name should describe the contents of a workbook. It can have up to eight characters.

Period

A period must separate the name and the extension.

Extension

The extension describes the type of information a workbook contains. It can have up to three characters.

48

You should give your workbook a descriptive name to remind you of the information it contains.

A file name *can* contain the following characters:

◆ The letters A to Z, upper or lower case

◆ The numbers 0 to 9

◆ The symbols
_ ^ $ ~ ! # % & { } @ ( )

A file name *cannot* contain the following characters:

◆ A comma (,)

◆ A blank space

◆ The symbols
* ? ; [ ] + = \ / : < >

Each file in a directory must have a unique name.

income94.xls
report.xls
taxes.xls

SAVE A WORKBOOK

SAVE A WORKBOOK

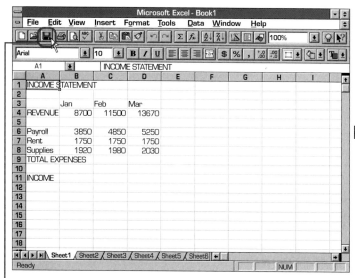

1 Move the mouse ⌖ over 🖫 and then press the left button.

*Note: If you previously saved your workbook, the **Save As** dialog box will **not** appear since you have already named the file.*

50

You should save your workbook to store it for future use.

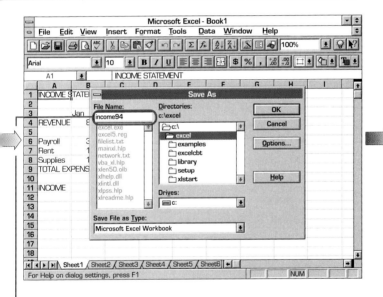

◆ The **Save As** dialog box appears.

2 Type a name for your workbook (example: **income94**) and then press **Enter**.

◆ To make it easier to find your workbook later on, do not type an extension. Excel will automatically add the **xls** extension to the file name.

To continue, refer to the next page.

SAVE A WORKBOOK (CONTINUED)

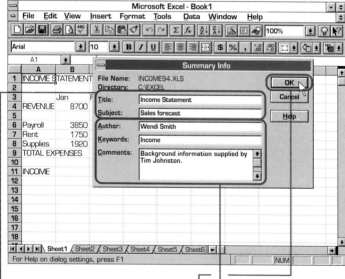

◆ The **Summary Info** dialog box appears.

3 Type a title for your workbook.

4 Press **Tab** to move to the next category. Type the corresponding information.

5 Repeat step **4** until you have typed all the information.

6 Move the mouse over **OK** and then press the left button.

52

Saving a workbook enables you to later retrieve the workbook for reviewing or editing purposes.

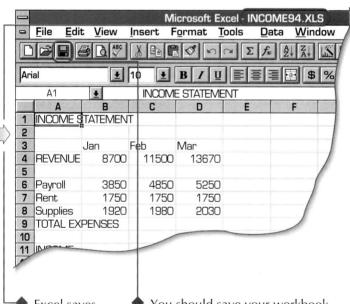

◆ Excel saves your workbook and displays the name at the top of your screen.

◆ You should save your workbook every 5 to 10 minutes to store any changes made since the last time you saved the workbook. To save changes, move the mouse ⌀ over 🖬 and then press the left button.

SAVE A WORKBOOK TO A DISKETTE

SAVE A WORKBOOK TO A DISKETTE

Today's Disk

1 Insert a diskette into a floppy drive (example: **drive a**).

As a precaution, you should save your workbook to a diskette. You can then use this copy to replace any lost data if your hard drive fails or you accidentally erase the file.

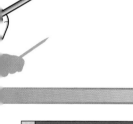

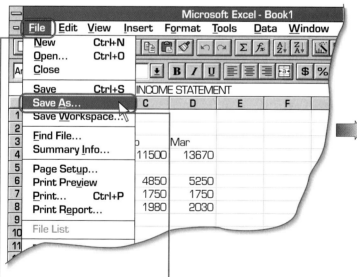

2 Move the mouse ▷ over **File** and then press the left button.

3 Move the mouse ▷ over **Save As** and then press the left button.

To continue, refer to the next page.

SAVE A WORKBOOK TO A DISKETTE

You can transfer a workbook to another computer by saving it to a diskette.

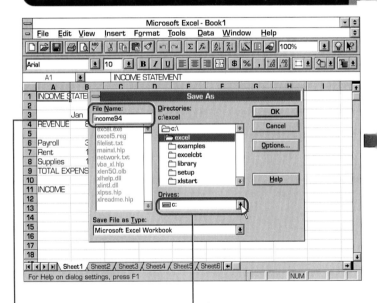

◆ The **Save As** dialog box appears.

4 The **File Name**: box displays the current file name. To save your workbook with a different name, type a new name.

◆ The **Drives**: box displays the current drive (example: **c:**).

5 To save the file to a different drive, move the mouse ⌖ over 🔽 in the **Drives**: box and then press the left button.

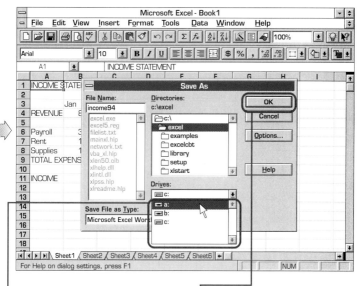

◆ A list of the available drives for your computer appears.

6 Move the mouse ⌖ over the drive you want to use (example: **a:**) and then press the left button.

7 To save your workbook, move the mouse ⌖ over **OK** and then press the left button.

EXIT EXCEL

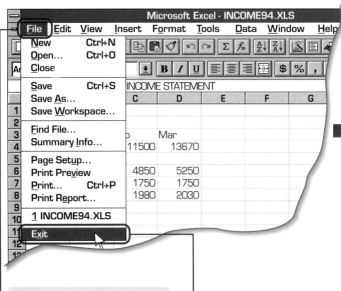

1 To exit Excel, move the mouse ⤵ over **File** and then press the left button.

2 Move the mouse ⤵ over **Exit** and then press the left button.

When you
finish using Excel,
you can exit the program
to return to the Windows
Program Manager.

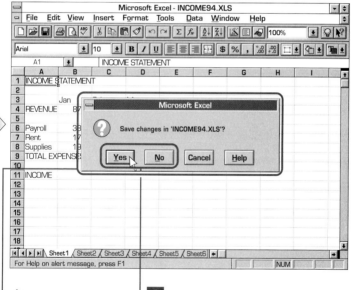

◆ This dialog box
appears if you have
not saved changes
made to your
workbook.

3 To save your workbook before
exiting, move the mouse ⅍ over **Yes**
and then press the left button.

◆ To exit without saving your
workbook, move the mouse ⅍ over
No and then press the left button.

OPEN A WORKBOOK

OPEN A WORKBOOK

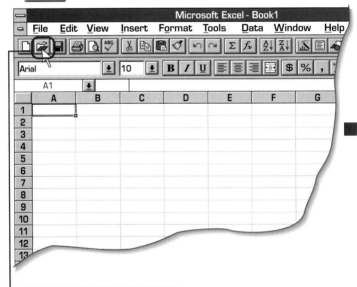

1 Move the mouse over 📂 and then press the left button.

◆ The **Open** dialog box appears.

> You can
> open a saved workbook
> and display it on
> your screen.

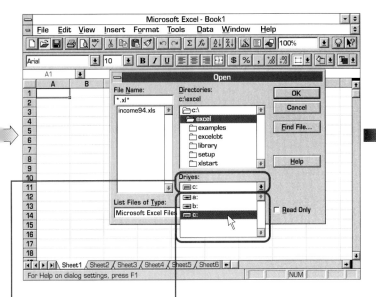

◆ The **Drives**: box displays the current drive (example: **c:**).

2 To open a file on a different drive, move the mouse ⇗ over ⬇ in the **Drives**: box and then press the left button.

◆ A list of the available drives for your computer appears.

3 Move the mouse ⇗ over the drive containing the file you want to open and then press the left button.

To continue, refer to the next page.

OPEN A WORKBOOK

OPEN A WORKBOOK (CONTINUED)

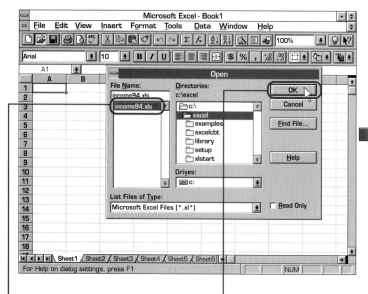

4 Move the mouse ⌖ over the name of the file you want to open (example: **income94.xls**) and then press the left button.

5 Move the mouse ⌖ over **OK** and then press the left button.

OPEN A WORKBOOK

OPEN A WORKBOOK (CONTINUED)

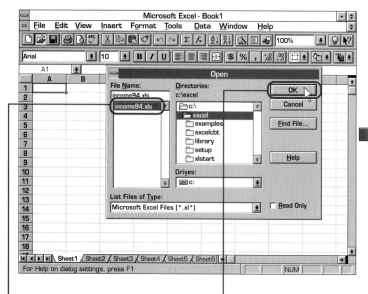

4 Move the mouse ⌖ over the name of the file you want to open (example: **income94.xls**) and then press the left button.

5 Move the mouse ⌖ over **OK** and then press the left button.

> Once
> you open
> a workbook, you can
> review and edit
> your work.

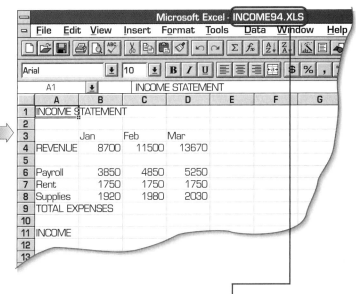

◆ Excel opens the workbook and displays it on your screen. You can now make changes to the workbook.

◆ The name of the workbook appears at the top of your screen.

OPEN A WORKBOOK

QUICKLY OPEN A WORKBOOK

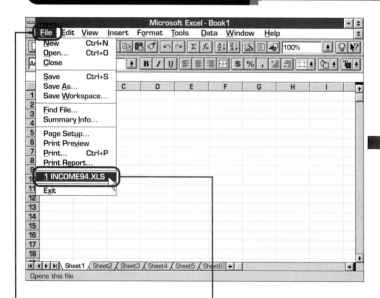

1 Move the mouse ⌖ over **File** and then press the left button.

2 Move the mouse ⌖ over the name of the workbook you want to open (example: **INCOME94.XLS**) and then press the left button.

Note: In this example, only one workbook has been opened.

The File menu displays the names of the last four workbooks you opened. You can easily open one of these workbooks.

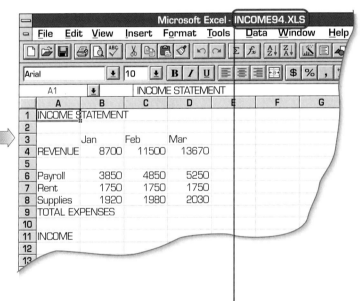

◆ Excel opens the workbook and displays it on your screen. You can now make changes to the workbook.

◆ The name of the workbook appears at the top of your screen.

EDIT DATA IN A CELL

EDIT DATA IN A CELL

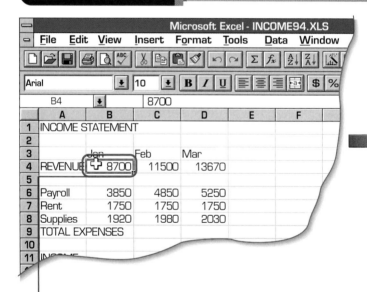

Microsoft Excel - INCOME94.XLS

File   Edit   View   Insert   Format   Tools   Data   Window

Arial   10   B   I   U $ %

B4   8700

	A	B	C	D	E	F
1	INCOME STATEMENT					
2						
3		Jan	Feb	Mar		
4	REVENUE	8700	11500	13670		
5						
6	Payroll	3850	4850	5250		
7	Rent	1750	1750	1750		
8	Supplies	1920	1980	2030		
9	TOTAL EXPENSES					
10						
11	INCOME					

1 Move the mouse ⊹ over the cell containing the data you want to change (example: **B4**) and then quickly press the left button twice.

After you enter data into your worksheet, you can correct a typing error or revise the data.

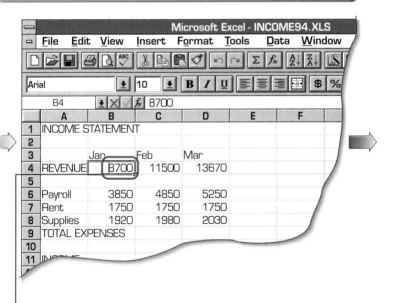

◆ A flashing insertion point appears in the cell.

2 Move the mouse ⅈ over the position where you want to add or delete characters and then press the left button.

◆ You can also press → or ← on your keyboard to move the insertion point.

To continue, refer to the next page.

67

EDIT DATA IN A CELL

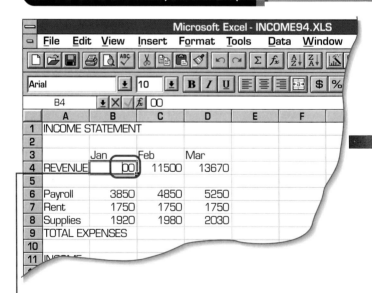

3 To remove the character to the right of the insertion point, press `Delete`.

◆ To remove the character to the left of the insertion point, press `←Backspace`.

REPLACE ENTIRE CELL CONTENTS

You can completely replace the contents of a cell with new data.

1 Move the mouse ⊕ over the cell containing the data you want to replace with new data and then press the left button.

2 Type the new data and then press `Enter`.

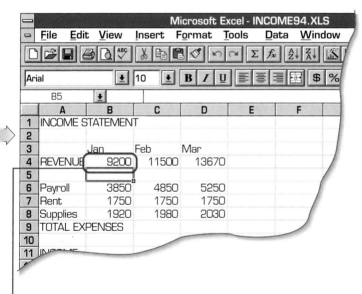

4 To insert data where the insertion point flashes on your screen, type the data.

5 When you finish making the changes, press `Enter`.

69

CLEAR DATA

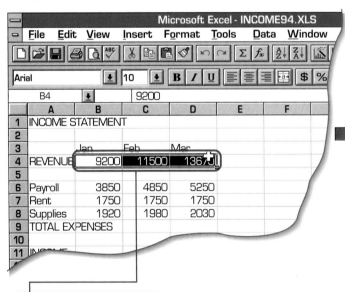

	Microsoft Excel - INCOME94.XLS					

File Edit View Insert Format Tools Data Window

Arial ▼ 10 ▼ **B** *I* <u>U</u> ≡ ≡ ≡ ⊞ $ %

	B4	▼	9200			
	A	B	C	D	E	F
1	INCOME STATEMENT					
2						
3		Jan	Feb	Mar		
4	REVENUE	9200	11500	13675		
5						
6	Payroll	3850	4850	5250		
7	Rent	1750	1750	1750		
8	Supplies	1920	1980	2030		
9	TOTAL EXPENSES					
10						
11	INCOME					

1 Select the cells containing the data you want to remove.

Note: To select cells, refer to pages 22 to 25.

70

You can completely erase the contents of cells in your worksheet.

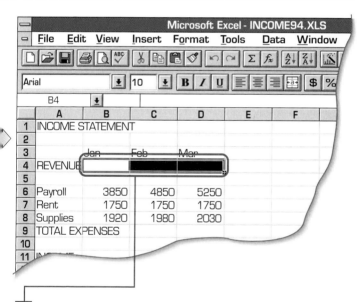

Microsoft Excel - INCOME94.XLS

| | File | Edit | View | Insert | Format | Tools | Data | Window |

Arial 10 B I U $ %

B4

	A	B	C	D	E	F
1	INCOME STATEMENT					
2						
3		Jan	Feb	Mar		
4	REVENUE					
5						
6	Payroll	3850	4850	5250		
7	Rent	1750	1750	1750		
8	Supplies	1920	1980	2030		
9	TOTAL EXPENSES					
10						
11						

2 Press Delete and the contents of the cells you selected disappear.

71

UNDO LAST CHANGE

Excel remembers the last change you made to your worksheet. If you regret this change, you can cancel it by using the Undo feature.

UNDO YOUR LAST CHANGE

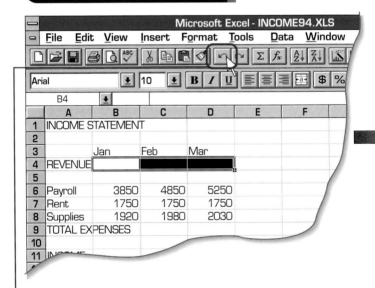

1 To cancel the last change made to your worksheet, move the mouse � over  and then press the left button.

72

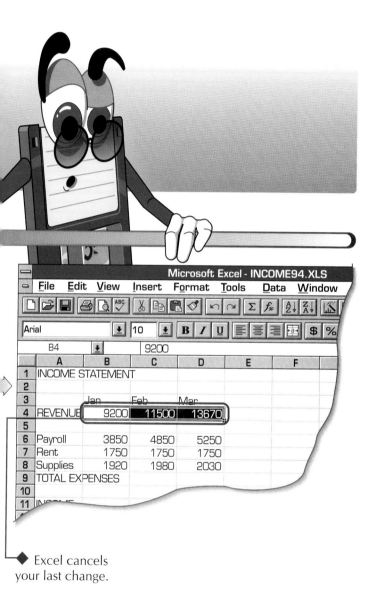

Microsoft Excel - INCOME94.XLS

File   Edit   View   Insert   Format   Tools   Data   Window

Arial   ▼   10   ▼   B   I   U   ≡ ≡ ≡ ⊞ $ %

B4   ▼   9200

	A	B	C	D	E	F
1	INCOME STATEMENT					
2						
3		Jan	Feb	Mar		
4	REVENUE	9200	11500	13670		
5						
6	Payroll	3850	4850	5250		
7	Rent	1750	1750	1750		
8	Supplies	1920	1980	2030		
9	TOTAL EXPENSES					
10						
11	INCOME					

◆ Excel cancels
your last change.

73

MOVE DATA

DRAG AND DROP DATA

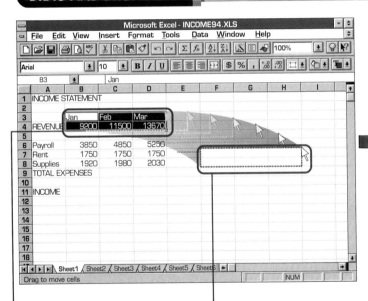

1 Select the cells containing the data you want to move to a new location.

Note: To select cells, refer to pages 22 to 25.

2 Move the mouse ⊹ over any border of the selected cells and ⊹ changes to ⬚.

3 Press and hold down the left button and then drag the mouse ⬚ where you want to place the data.

◆ A rectangular box indicates where the data will appear.

You can use the Drag and Drop feature to move data from one location in your worksheet to another. The original data disappears.

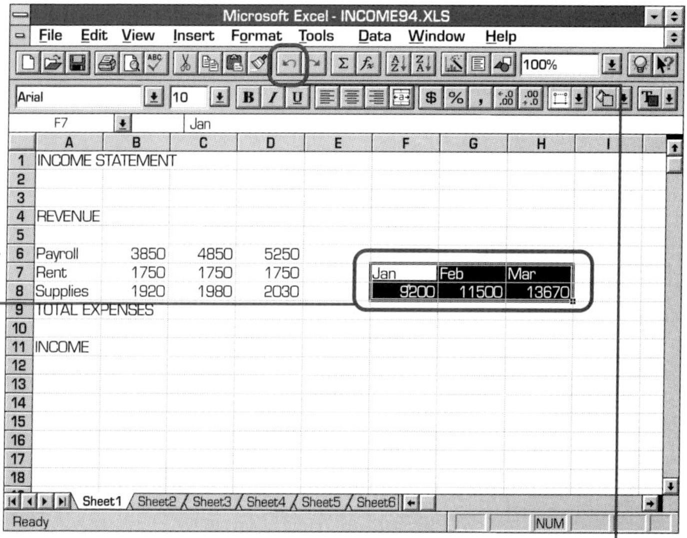

4 Release the left button and the data moves to the new location.

CANCEL THE MOVE

◆ To immediately cancel the move, position the mouse over the Undo button and then press the left button.

MOVE DATA

The Cut and Paste features let you move data from one location in your worksheet to another. The original data disappears.

CUT AND PASTE DATA

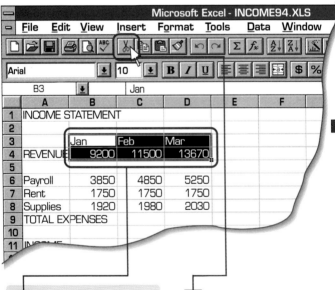

1 Select the cells containing the data you want to move to a new location.

Note: To select cells, refer to pages 22 to 25.

2 Move the mouse ⌖ over ✂ and then press the left button.

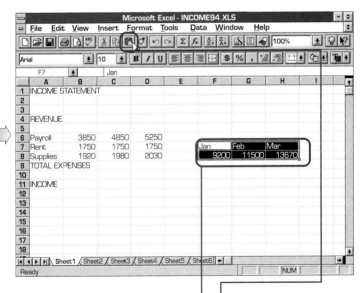

3 Select the cell where you want to place the data (example: **F7**). This cell will become the top left cell of the new location.

4 Move the mouse ⇧ over 🗐 and then press the left button.

◆ The data appears in the new location.

COPY DATA

You can use the Drag and Drop feature to copy data from one location in your worksheet to another. The original data remains in its place.

DRAG AND DROP DATA

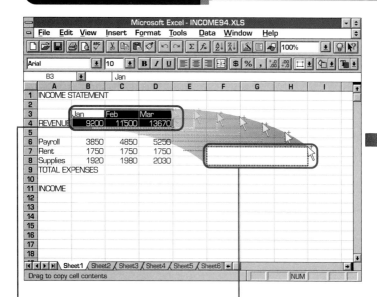

1 Select the cells containing the data you want to copy to a new location.

2 Move the mouse ⊕ over any border of the selected cells (⊕ changes to ↖).

3 Press and hold down **Ctrl** and the left button (↖ changes to ↖).

4 Still holding down **Ctrl** and the left button, drag the mouse ↖ where you want to place the data.

◆ A rectangular box indicates where the data will appear.

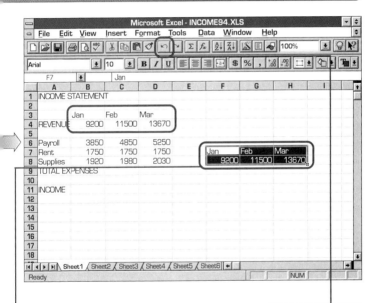

5 Release the left button and then release Ctrl.

◆ A copy of the data appears in the new location.

CANCEL THE COPY

◆ To immediately cancel the copy, position the mouse ⓚ over 🔙 and then press the left button.

COPY DATA

COPY AND PASTE DATA

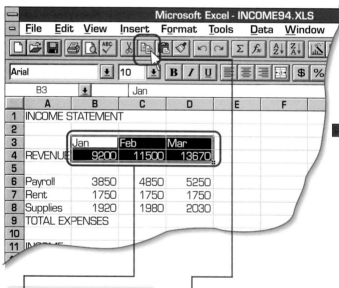

1 Select the cells containing the data you want to copy to a new location.

Note: To select cells, refer to pages 22 to 25.

2 Move the mouse ⌖ over 🗐 and then press the left button.

The Copy and Paste features let you copy data from one location in your worksheet to another. The original data remains in its place.

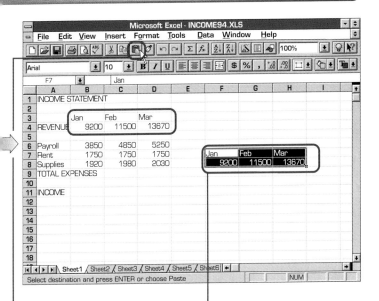

3 Select the cell where you want to place the data (example: **F7**). This cell will become the top left cell of the new location.

4 Move the mouse over 🖹 and then press the left button.

◆ A copy of the data appears in the new location.

Note: You can repeat steps **3** *and* **4** *to place the data in multiple locations in your worksheet.*

CHECK SPELLING

You can use Excel's Spelling feature to find and correct spelling errors in your worksheet.

CHECK SPELLING

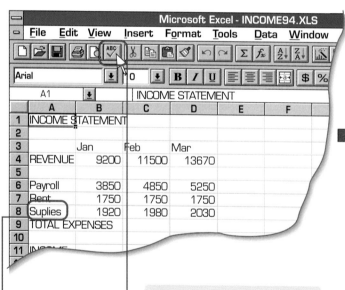

◆ In this example, the letter **p** was removed from **Supplies**.

1 To start the spell check at the beginning of your worksheet, press Ctrl + Home to move to cell **A1**.

2 Move the mouse ⌖ over 🗹 and then press the left button.

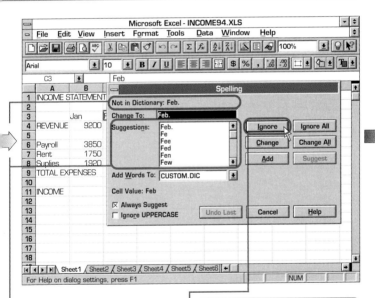

◆ If Excel finds a spelling error, the **Spelling** dialog box appears.

◆ Excel displays the word it does not recognize and suggestions to correct the error.

Ignore misspelled word

3 If you do not want to change the spelling of the word, move the mouse ⇗ over **Ignore** and then press the left button.

To continue, refer to the next page.

83

CHECK SPELLING

Excel compares every word in your worksheet to words in its own dictionary. If a word does not exist in the dictionary, Excel considers it misspelled.

CHECK SPELLING (CONTINUED)

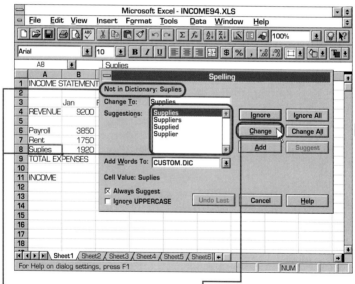

Correct misspelled word

◆ Excel displays the next word it does not recognize.

4 To correct the spelling, move the mouse ⌖ over the word you want to use and then press the left button.

5 To replace the misspelled word in your worksheet with the correct spelling, move the mouse ⌖ over **Change** and then press the left button.

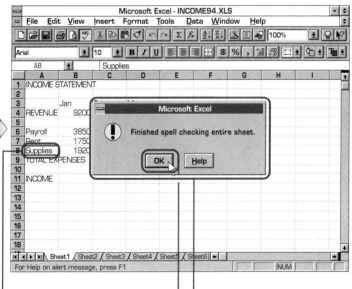

◆ Excel corrects the word and continues checking for spelling errors.

6 Ignore or correct spelling errors until Excel finishes checking your worksheet.

◆ This dialog box appears when the spell check is complete.

7 To close the dialog box, move the mouse ⌖ over **OK** and then press the left button.

FORMULAS

$$3.14 \, c \, (3a \times 700) \div 1,298 - .654$$
$$89 \quad 32 \times \frac{6.78 \div 508^{10}}{2309}$$
$$4 \quad 6b \div 98.08 \sqrt{45.76}$$

INTRODUCTION TO FORMULAS

You can use the following operators in your formulas:	
+	Addition
-	Subtraction
*	Multiplication
/	Division
^	Exponentiation

◆ You must always begin a formula with an equal sign (=).

◆ You should use cell references (example: **A1**) instead of actual numbers whenever possible. This way, if your data changes, Excel will automatically redo the calculations.

You can use formulas to perform calculations on your worksheet data.

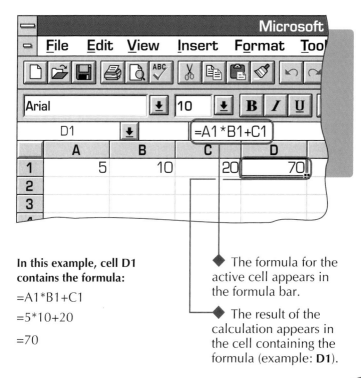

In this example, cell **D1** contains the formula:

=A1*B1+C1

=5*10+20

=70

◆ The formula for the active cell appears in the formula bar.

◆ The result of the calculation appears in the cell containing the formula (example: **D1**).

87

FORMULAS

INTRODUCTION TO FORMULAS

◆ Excel will perform calculations in the following order:

1 Exponentiation

2 Multiplication and Division

3 Addition and Subtraction

You can change this order by using parentheses ( ).

Excel will perform all of your calculations in a specific order.

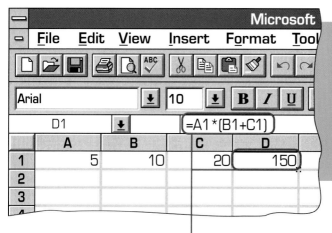

Excel will calculate the numbers in parentheses first.

◆ In this example, cell D1 contains the formula:

=A1*(B1+C1)

=5*(10+20)

=150

ENTER A FORMULA

ENTER A FORMULA

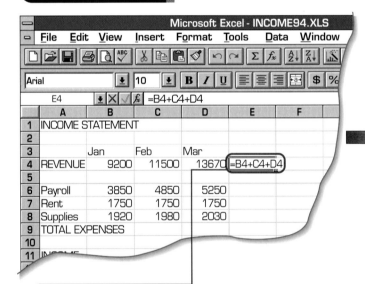

1 Move the mouse ⇧ over the cell where you want to enter a formula (example: **E4**) and then press the left button.

2 Type an equal sign (=) to begin the formula.

3 Type the calculation you want to perform (example: **B4+C4+D4**).

Note: This formula will calculate the total Revenue.

You can enter a formula into any cell in your worksheet.

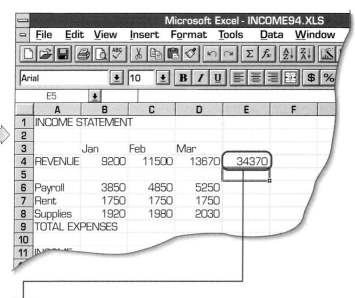

4 Press **Enter** and the result of the calculation appears in the cell (example: **34370**).

AUTOMATIC RECALCULATION

AUTOMATIC RECALCULATION

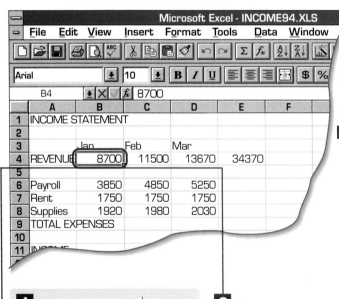

1 Move the mouse ⊕ over the cell containing the number you want to change (example: **B4**) and then press the left button.

2 Type a new number (example: **8700**).

If you change a number used in a formula, Excel will automatically calculate a new result.

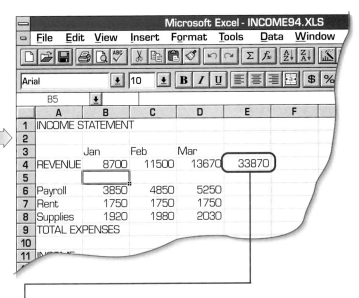

3 Press **Enter** and Excel automatically recalculates the formula using the new number.

FUNCTIONS

INTRODUCTION TO FUNCTIONS

◆ A function starts with an equal sign (=).

◆ You should use cell references (example: **A1**) instead of actual numbers whenever possible. This way, if your data changes, Excel will automatically redo the calculations.

> A function is a ready-to-use formula. Excel offers over 300 functions that you can use to perform calculations on data in your worksheet.

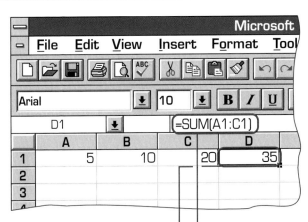

In this example, cell D1 contains the function:

=SUM(A1:C1)

=A1+B1+C1

=5+10+20

=35

◆ The function for the active cell appears in the formula bar.

◆ The result of the calculation appears in the cell containing the function (example: **D1**).

95

FUNCTIONS

You must tell Excel what data to use to calculate a function. This data is enclosed in parentheses ( ).

$$=SUM(A1,A3,A5)$$

◆ When there is a comma (,) between cell references in a function, Excel uses each cell to perform the calculation.

Example: =SUM(A1,A3,A5) is the same as the formula =A1+A3+A5.

$$=SUM(A1:A4)$$

◆ When there is a colon (:) between cell references in a function, Excel uses the displayed cells and all cells between them to perform the calculation.

Example: =SUM(A1:A4) is the same as the formula =A1+A2+A3+A4.

Common Functions		
AVERAGE	Calculates the average value of a list of numbers.	
	Example: =AVERAGE(B1:B6)	
COUNT	Counts the number of values in a list of numbers.	
	Example: =COUNT(B1:B6)	
MAX	Finds the largest value in a list of numbers.	
	Example: =MAX(B1:B6)	
MIN	Finds the smallest value in a list of numbers.	
	Example: =MIN(B1:B6)	
ROUND	Rounds a number to a specific number of digits.	
	Example: =ROUND(B6,2)	
SUM	Adds a list of numbers.	
	Example: =SUM(B1:B6)	

ENTER A FUNCTION

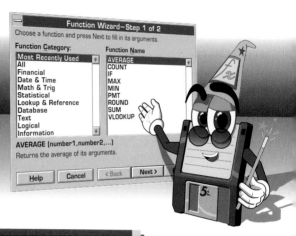

 ENTER A FUNCTION

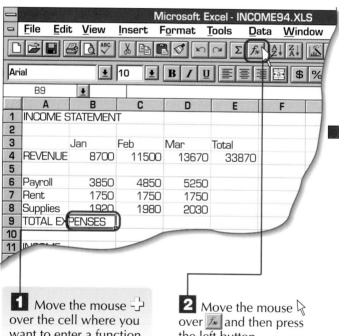

1 Move the mouse ⊹ over the cell where you want to enter a function (example: **B9**) and then press the left button.

2 Move the mouse ⌖ over ƒx and then press the left button.

The Function Wizard lets you perform calculations without typing long, complex formulas.

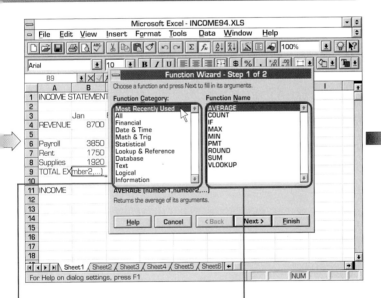

◆ The **Function Wizard** dialog box appears.

3 Move the mouse ⏳ over the category containing the function you want to use and then press the left button.

*Note: If you do not know which category contains the function you want to use, select **All**. This will display a list of all the functions.*

◆ This area displays the functions in the category you selected.

To continue, refer to the next page.

99

ENTER A FUNCTION

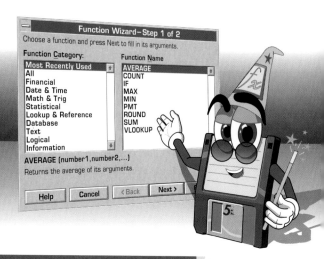

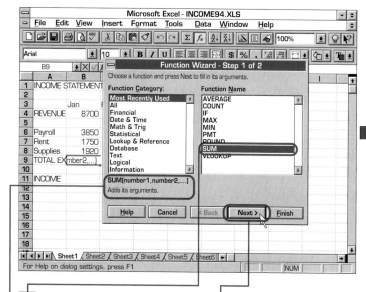

4 Move the mouse ⌐ over the function you want to use (example: **SUM**) and then press the left button.

◆ A description of the function you selected appears.

5 To select the function, move the mouse ⌐ over **Next** and then press the left button.

You can select from hundreds of functions to perform tasks such as averaging a group of numbers or calculating mortgage payments.

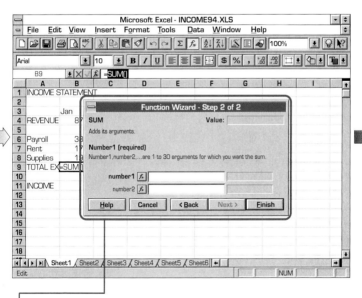

◆ This dialog box appears. The text in the dialog box depends on the function you selected in step **4**.

To continue, refer to the next page.

101

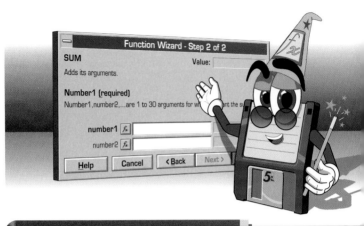

ENTER A FUNCTION (CONTINUED)

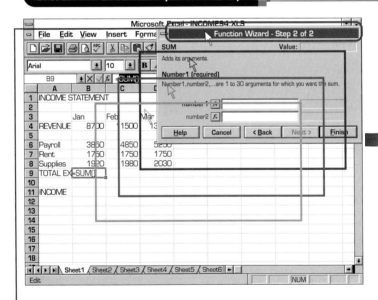

6 To move the dialog box, position the mouse ⌖ over the title bar and then press and hold down the left button.

7 Still holding down the button, drag the box to a new location.

If the Function Wizard dialog box covers the data you want to use in the function, you can move it to another location on your screen.

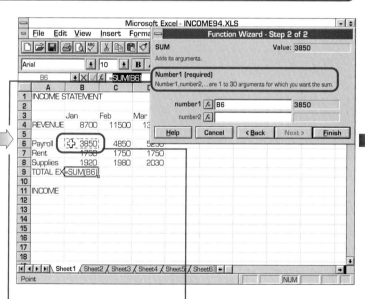

8 Release the button and the dialog box moves to the new location.

◆ This area describes the first number Excel needs to perform the function.

9 To select a number, move the mouse over the cell containing the data you want to use and then press the left button.

◆ If the number you want to enter does not appear in your worksheet, type the number.

To continue, refer to the next page.

103

ENTER A FUNCTION

If you change a number used in a function, Excel will automatically calculate a new result.

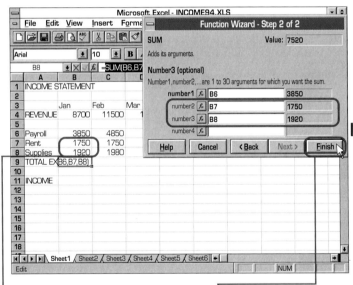

10 To display a description of the next number Excel needs to perform the function, press `Tab`.

11 Repeat steps **9** and **10** starting on page 103 until you have selected all the cells you want to use in the function.

12 Move the mouse ⌖ over **Finish** and then press the left button.

TIP

◆ In the example below, you can quickly enter numbers in the **Function Wizard** dialog box. Replace steps **9** to **11** starting on page 103 by selecting cells **B6** to **B8**.

Note: To select cells, refer to pages 24 to 25.

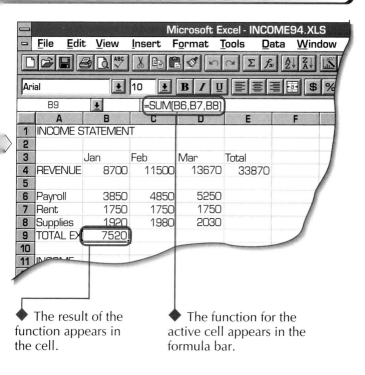

◆ The result of the function appears in the cell.

◆ The function for the active cell appears in the formula bar.

ADD NUMBERS

ADD A LIST OF NUMBERS

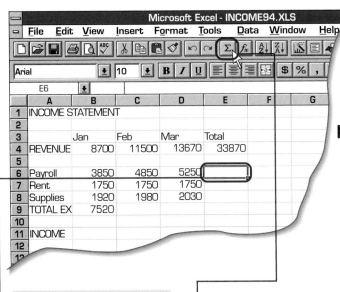

1 Move the mouse ✛ over the cell you want to display the sum (example: **E6**) and then press the left button.

2 Move the mouse ↖ over Σ and then press the left button.

Note: Σ is the Greek symbol for sum.

You can use the AutoSum feature to quickly add a list of numbers in your worksheet.

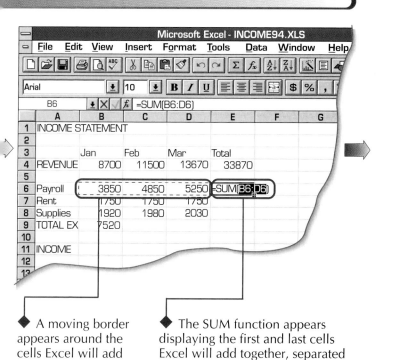

◆ A moving border appears around the cells Excel will add together.

◆ The SUM function appears displaying the first and last cells Excel will add together, separated by a colon (:).

◆ To add a different list of cells, select the cells. To select cells, refer to pages 22 to 25.

To continue, refer to the next page.

ADD NUMBERS

ADD A LIST OF NUMBERS (CONTINUED)

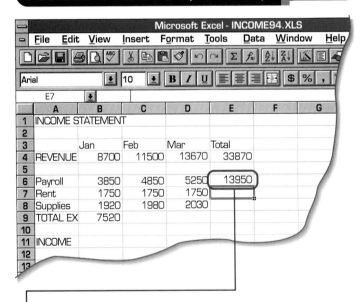

3 Press **Enter** and the result appears in the cell.

The AutoSum feature will also add several lists of numbers at the same time.

ADD SEVERAL LISTS OF NUMBERS

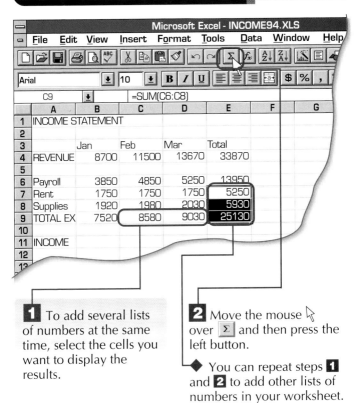

1 To add several lists of numbers at the same time, select the cells you want to display the results.

2 Move the mouse ⬚ over Σ and then press the left button.

◆ You can repeat steps **1** and **2** to add other lists of numbers in your worksheet.

109

ERRORS IN FORMULAS

#DIV/0!	This error appears in a cell if the formula you entered divides a number by zero.

	A	B	C	D
1	50		35	
2	0			
3	#DIV/0!		#DIV/0!	
4				
5				

This cell contains the formula =A1/A2 =50/0

The formula divides a number by 0.

This cell contains the formula =C1/C2 =35/0

The formula divides a number by 0.

Note: Excel considers a blank cell to contain the zero value.

An error message appears when Excel cannot properly calculate a formula.

#NAME?

This error appears in a cell if the formula you entered contains a name that Excel does not recognize.

	A	B	C	D
1	5		30	
2	10		5	
3	20		10	
4	#NAME?		#NAME?	
5				

This cell contains the formula =A1+A2A3

The formula is missing a plus sign (+).

This cell contains the function =SUMM(C1:C3)

The name of the function is misspelled.

111

ERRORS IN FORMULAS

COMMON ERRORS IN FORMULAS

#REF!

This error appears in a cell if the formula you entered refers to a cell that is not valid.

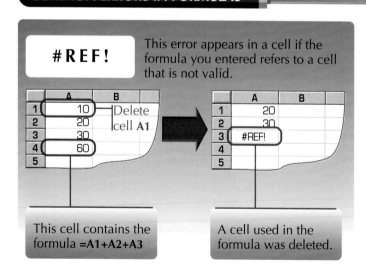

This cell contains the formula =A1+A2+A3

A cell used in the formula was deleted.

You can correct an error by editing the cell displaying the error message.

CORRECT AN ERROR

1 To correct an error, move the mouse ⊹ over the cell displaying the error message and then quickly press the left button twice.

2 Correct the error by editing the formula as you would any data in your worksheet.

Note: To edit data, refer to pages 66 to 69.

COPY FORMULAS

After entering a formula in your worksheet, you can copy the formula to other cells.

COPY FORMULAS (USING RELATIVE REFERENCES)

When you copy a formula, Excel automatically changes the cell references in the formula.

	A	B	C	
1	10	20	5	
2	20	30	10	
3	30	40	20	
4	60	90	35	
5				
6				

=A1+A2+A3 ➡ =B1+B2+B3   =C1+C2+C3

This cell contains the formula =A1+A2+A3

If you copy the formula to other cells in the worksheet, the cell references in the new formulas automatically change.

1 Type and enter the formula you want to copy to other cells (example: **=B4-B9** in cell **B11** to calculate INCOME).

2 Move the mouse over the cell containing the formula (example: **B11**) and then press the left button.

To continue, refer to the next page.

115

COPY FORMULAS

Copying a formula to other cells in your worksheet can save you time.

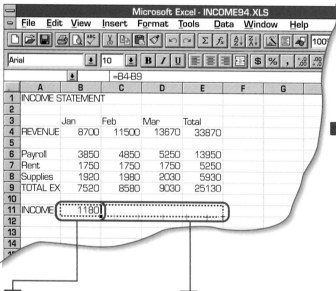

3 Move the mouse ⌘ over the bottom right corner of the cell and ⌘ changes to +.

4 Press and hold down the left button as you drag the mouse + over the cells you want to receive a copy of the formula.

Microsoft Excel - INCOME94.XLS

File   Edit   View   Insert   Format   Tools   Data   Window   Help

Arial   10   B   I   U $ %

B11   =B4-B9

	A	B	C	D	E	F	G
1	INCOME STATEMENT						
2							
3		Jan	Feb	Mar	Total		
4	REVENUE	8700	11500	13670	33870		
5							
6	Payroll	3850	4850	5250	13950		
7	Rent	1750	1750	1750	5250		
8	Supplies	1920	1980	2030	5930		
9	TOTAL EX	7520	8580	9030	25130		
10							
11	INCOME	1180	2920	4640	8740		
12							
13							
14							
15							

5 Release the button and
the results of the formulas
appear.

COPY FORMULAS

COPY FORMULAS (USING ABSOLUTE REFERENCES)

To make a cell reference absolute, type a dollar sign ($) before both the column letter and row number (example: $B$1).

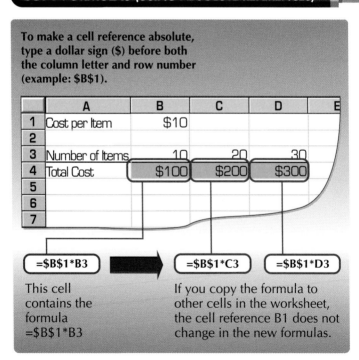

	A	B	C	D	E
1	Cost per Item	$10			
2					
3	Number of Items	10	20	30	
4	Total Cost	$100	$200	$300	
5					
6					
7					

=$B$1*B3 ➡ =$B$1*C3   =$B$1*D3

This cell contains the formula =$B$1*B3

If you copy the formula to other cells in the worksheet, the cell reference B1 does not change in the new formulas.

You can copy a formula to other cells in your worksheet. If you do not want Excel to change a cell reference, you must lock the reference when copying the formula. A locked cell reference is called an absolute reference.

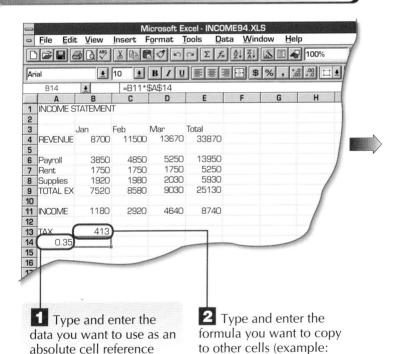

1 Type and enter the data you want to use as an absolute cell reference (example: **0.35** in cell **A14**).

2 Type and enter the formula you want to copy to other cells (example: =B11*$A$14 in cell B13).

To continue, refer to the next page.

119

COPY FORMULAS

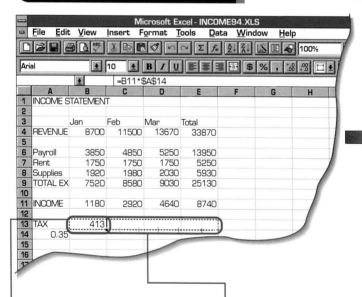

3 Move the mouse ⊹ over the cell containing the formula you want to copy (example: **B13**) and then press the left button.

4 Move the mouse ⊹ over the bottom right corner of the cell and ⊹ changes to **+**.

5 Press and hold down the left button as you drag the mouse **+** over the cells you want to receive a copy of the formula.

An absolute reference always refers to the same cell, regardless of where you copy the formula.

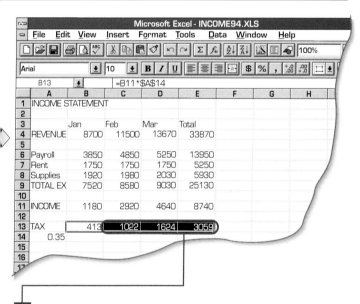

6 Release the button and the results of the formulas appear.

121

INSERT A ROW

You can add a row to your worksheet if you want to insert new data.

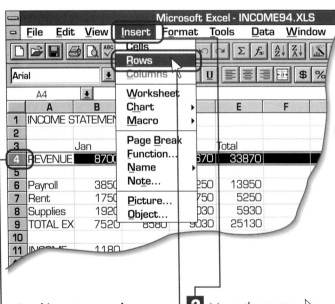

Microsoft Excel - INCOME94.XLS

File Edit View Insert Format Tools Data Window

Insert menu:
- Cells
- **Rows**
- Columns
- Worksheet
- Chart ▶
- Macro ▶
- Page Break
- Function...
- Name ▶
- Note...
- Picture...
- Object...

	A	B			E	F
1	INCOME STATEMEN					
2						
3		Jan			Total	
4	REVENUE	870			670	33870
5						
6	Payroll	3850			250	13950
7	Rent	1750			750	5250
8	Supplies	1920			030	5930
9	TOTAL EX	7520	8580	9030	25130	
10						
11	INCOME	1180				

Excel inserts a row above the row you select.

1 To select a row, move the mouse ⊕ over the row heading (example: **row 4**) and then press the left button.

2 Move the mouse ⌖ over **Insert** and then press the left button.

3 Move the mouse ⌖ over **Rows** and then press the left button.

122

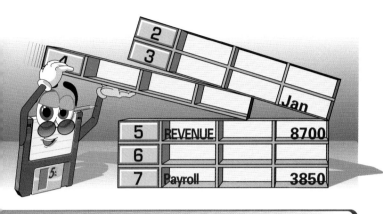

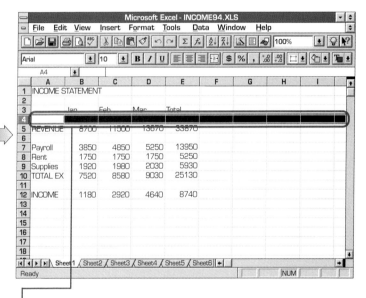

◆ The new row appears
and all the rows that follow
shift downward.

INSERT A COLUMN

INSERT A COLUMN

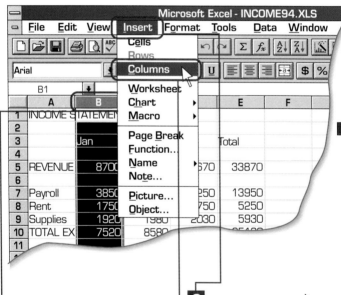

Excel inserts a column to the left of the column you select.

1 To select a column, move the mouse ⇩ over the column heading (example: **column B**) and then press the left button.

2 Move the mouse ⇩ over **Insert** and then press the left button.

3 Move the mouse ⇩ over **Columns** and then press the left button.

You can add a column to your worksheet at any time. The existing columns shift to make room for the new column.

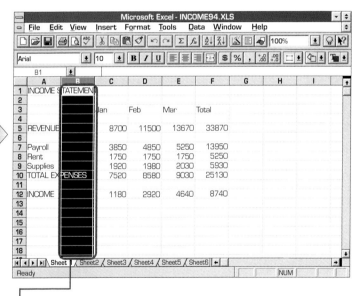

◆ The new column appears and all the columns that follow shift to the right.

DELETE A ROW OR COLUMN

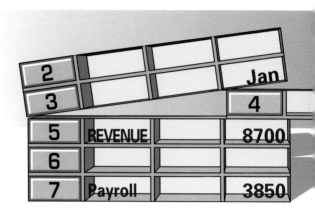

DELETE A ROW OR COLUMN

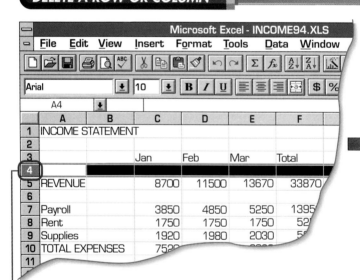

Microsoft Excel - INCOME94.XLS

File Edit View Insert Format Tools Data Window

Arial   10   B I U $ %

A4

	A	B	C	D	E	F
1	INCOME STATEMENT					
2						
3			Jan	Feb	Mar	Total
4						
5	REVENUE		8700	11500	13670	33870
6						
7	Payroll		3850	4850	5250	1395
8	Rent		1750	1750	1750	52
9	Supplies		1920	1980	2030	5
10	TOTAL EXPENSES		752			
11						

1 To select a row you want to delete, move the mouse ⬦⊹ over the row heading (example: **row 4**) and then press the left button.

◆ To select a column you want to delete, move the mouse ⬦⊹ over the column heading (example: **column B**) and then press the left button.

126

You can delete a row or column from your worksheet. This lets you remove cells you no longer need.

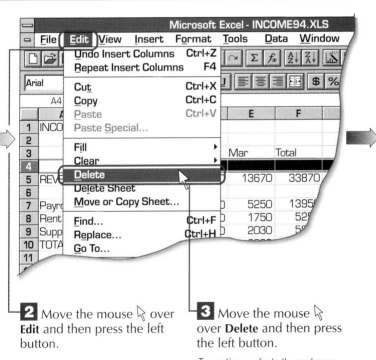

2 Move the mouse ⟍ over **Edit** and then press the left button.

3 Move the mouse ⟍ over **Delete** and then press the left button.

To continue, refer to the next page.

127

DELETE A ROW OR COLUMN

DELETE A ROW OR COLUMN (CONTINUED)

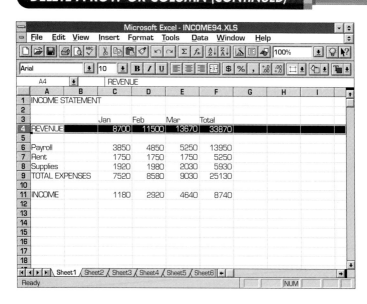

◆ The row or column
disappears from your
worksheet.

When you delete a row or column from your worksheet, the remaining rows or columns move to fill the empty space.

#REF!

If #REF! appears in a cell in your worksheet, you have deleted data needed to calculate a formula.

1 To immediately cancel the deletion, move the mouse ▷ over 🔲 and then press the left button.

CHANGE COLUMN WIDTH

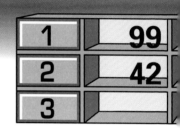

CHANGE COLUMN WIDTH

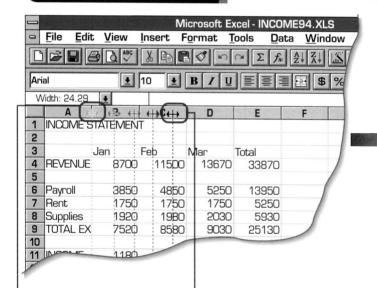

Microsoft Excel - INCOME94.XLS

| File | Edit | View | Insert | Format | Tools | Data | Window |

Arial · · 10 · · B I U ≡ ≡ ≡ 🔲 $ %

Width: 24.29 ▼

	A				D	E	F
1	INCOME STATEMENT						
2							
3		Jan	Feb	Mar	Total		
4	REVENUE	8700	11500	13670	33870		
5							
6	Payroll	3850	4850	5250	13950		
7	Rent	1750	1750	1750	5250		
8	Supplies	1920	1980	2030	5930		
9	TOTAL EX	7520	8580	9030	25130		
10							
11	INCOME	1180					

1 Move the mouse ⊹ over the right edge of the column heading you want to change (example: **column A**) and ⊹ changes to ↔.

2 Press and hold down the left button as you drag the edge of the column to a new position.

◆ A dotted line indicates the new column width.

You can improve the appearance of your worksheet and display hidden data by changing the width of columns.

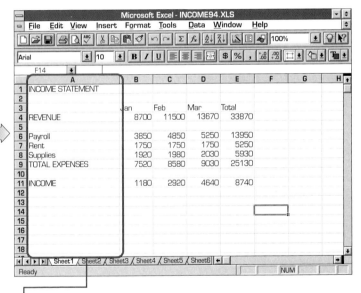

3 Release the button and the new column width appears.

CHANGE COLUMN WIDTH

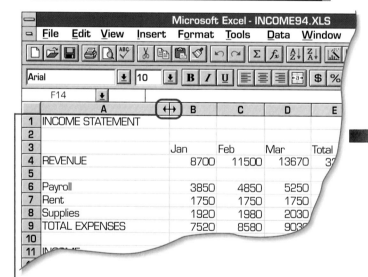

1 Move the mouse ⊕ over the right edge of the column heading you want to change (example: **column A**) and ⊕ changes to ↔.

2 Quickly press the left button twice.

You can have Excel adjust a column width to fit the longest item in the column.

◆ The column width changes to fit the longest item in the column.

CHANGE ROW HEIGHT

CHANGE ROW HEIGHT

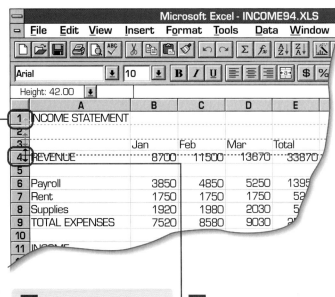

1 Move the mouse 🖑 over the bottom edge of the row heading you want to change (example: **row 1**) and 🖑 changes to ‡.

2 Press and hold down the left button as you drag the edge of the row to a new position.

◆ A dotted line indicates the new row height.

134

You can change the height of a row. This lets you display a title at the top of your worksheet or add space between rows of data.

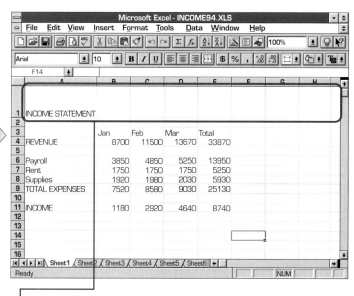

3 Release the button and the new row height appears.

CHANGE ROW HEIGHT

CHANGE ROW HEIGHT AUTOMATICALLY

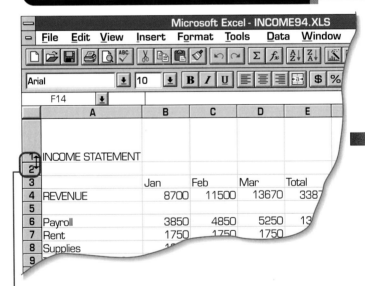

1 Move the mouse ⊹ over the bottom edge of the row heading you want to change (example: **row 1**) and ⊹ changes to ‡ .

2 Quickly press the left button twice.

136

You can have Excel adjust the row height to fit the tallest item in the row.

◆ The row height changes to fit the tallest item in the row.

137

CHANGE APPEARANCE OF NUMBERS

You can change the appearance of numbers in your worksheet without having to retype the numbers.

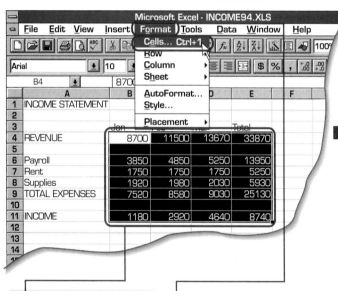

1 Select the cells containing the numbers you want to change.

Note: To select cells, refer to pages 22 to 25.

2 Move the mouse over **Format** and then press the left button.

3 Move the mouse over **Cells** and then press the left button.

138

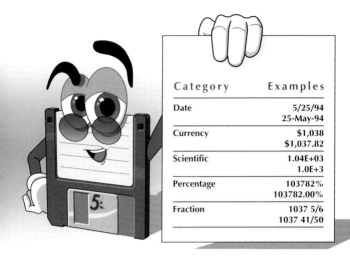

Category	Examples
Date	5/25/94
	25-May-94
Currency	$1,038
	$1,037.82
Scientific	1.04E+03
	1.0E+3
Percentage	103782%
	103782.00%
Fraction	1037 5/6
	1037 41/50

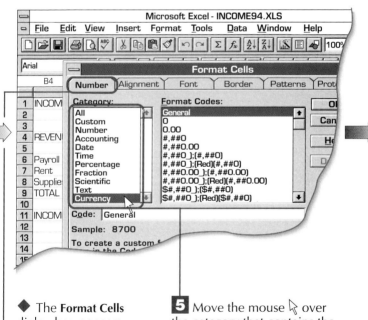

◆ The **Format Cells**
dialog box appears.

4 Move the mouse ⌖
over the **Number** tab and
then press the left button.

5 Move the mouse ⌖ over
the category that contains the
number style you want to use
(example: **Currency**) and then
press the left button.

*Note: The **All** option displays a list of
all the styles.*

To continue, refer to the next page.

139

CHANGE APPEARANCE OF NUMBERS

Changing the appearance of numbers in your worksheet can make the numbers easier to understand.

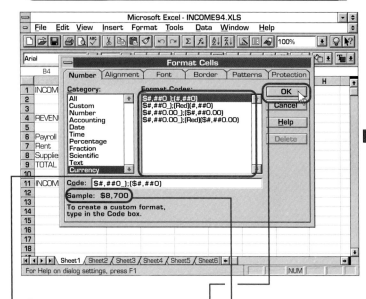

◆ This area displays the styles in the category you selected.

6 Move the mouse ⤢ over the style you want to use and then press the left button.

◆ This area displays a sample of the style you selected.

7 Move the mouse ⤢ over **OK** and then press the left button.

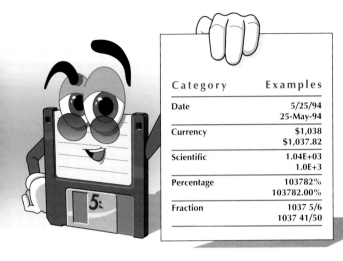

Category	Examples
Date	5/25/94
	25-May-94
Currency	$1,038
	$1,037.82
Scientific	1.04E+03
	1.0E+3
Percentage	103782%
	103782.00%
Fraction	1037 5/6
	1037 41/50

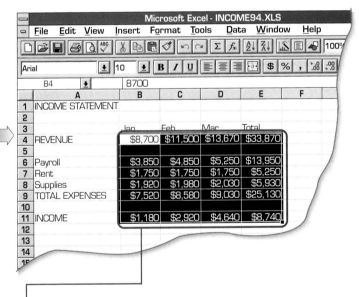

◆ The numbers in the cells you selected display the new style.

Note: If number signs (#) appear in a cell, the column is not wide enough to display the entire number. To change the column width, refer to page 130.

CHANGE APPEARANCE
OF NUMBERS

QUICKLY CHANGE APPEARANCE OF NUMBERS

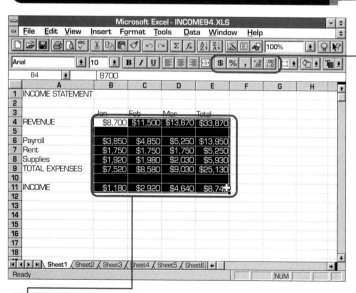

Microsoft Excel - INCOME94.XLS

File Edit View Insert Format Tools Data Window Help

	A	B	C	D	E	F	G	H
1	INCOME STATEMENT							
2								
3		Jan	Feb	Mar	Total			
4	REVENUE	$8,700	$11,500	$13,670	$33,870			
5								
6	Payroll	$3,850	$4,850	$5,250	$13,950			
7	Rent	$1,750	$1,750	$1,750	$5,250			
8	Supplies	$1,920	$1,980	$2,030	$5,930			
9	TOTAL EXPENSES	$7,520	$8,580	$9,030	$25,130			
10								
11	INCOME	$1,180	$2,920	$4,640	$8,74			
12								
13								
14								
15								
16								
17								
18								

Sheet1 Sheet2 Sheet3 Sheet4 Sheet5 Sheet6

Ready   NUM

1 Select the cells containing the numbers you want to change.

Note: To select cells, refer to pages 22 to 25.

142

Excel provides five buttons to quickly change the appearance of numbers in your worksheet.

2 Move the mouse ▷ over one of the following options and then press the left button.

$ Displays the number as a dollar value.
Example: 7147 ➜ $7,147.00

% Displays the number as a percentage.
Example: 0.35 ➜ 35%

, Adds a comma and two decimal places to the number.
Example: 2683 ➜ 2,683.00

⁺.0 .00 Adds one decimal place to the number.
Example: 52.3 ➜ 52.30

.00 ⁺.0 Deletes one decimal place from the number.
Example: 49.27 ➜ 49.3

ALIGN DATA

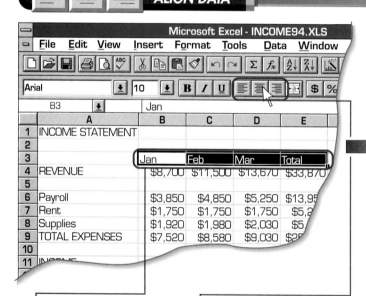

1 Select the cells containing the data you want to align.

Note: To select cells, refer to pages 22 to 25.

2 Move the mouse ⬚ over one of the following options and then press the left button.

⬚ Left align data

⬚ Center data

⬚ Right align data

You can change the position of data in each cell of your worksheet. Excel offers several alignment options.

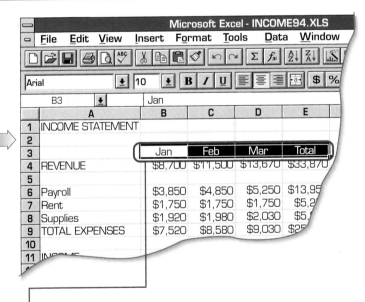

◆ The data in the cells you selected displays the new alignment.

Note: In this example, the data appears centered in the cells.

CENTER DATA ACROSS COLUMNS

> You can center data across columns in your worksheet. This is useful for displaying titles.

CENTER DATA ACROSS COLUMNS

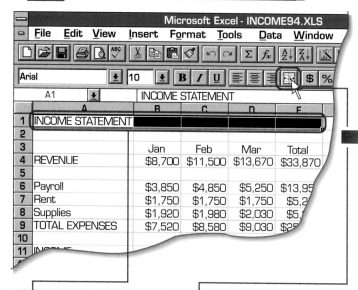

Microsoft Excel - INCOME94.XLS

File Edit View Insert Format Tools Data Window

Arial   10   B I U $ %

A1   INCOME STATEMENT

	A	B	C	D	E
1	INCOME STATEMENT				
2					
3		Jan	Feb	Mar	Total
4	REVENUE	$8,700	$11,500	$13,670	$33,870
5					
6	Payroll	$3,850	$4,850	$5,250	$13,95
7	Rent	$1,750	$1,750	$1,750	$5,2
8	Supplies	$1,920	$1,980	$2,030	$5,
9	TOTAL EXPENSES	$7,520	$8,580	$9,030	$2
10					
11	INCOME				

1 To center data across columns, select the cells you want to center the data between.

Note: For best results, the first cell you select should contain the data you want to center.

2 Move the mouse ⌨ over 🔳 and then press the left button.

146

	A	B	C	D	E
1		INCOME STATEMENT			
2					
3		Jan	Feb	Mar	Total
4	REVENUE	$8,700	$11,500	$13,670	$33,870
5					
6	Payroll	$3,850	$4,850	$5,250	$13,95
7	Rent	$1,750	$1,750	$1,750	$5,2
8	Supplies	$1,920	$1,980	$2,030	$5,
9	TOTAL EXPENSES	$7,520	$8,580	$9,030	$25
10					
11	INCOME				

Microsoft Excel - INCOME94.XLS

File   Edit   View   Insert   Format   Tools   Data   Window

Arial   10   B   I   U

A1   INCOME STATEMENT

◆ Excel displays the
data centered between
the cells you selected.

BOLD, ITALIC AND UNDERLINE

> You can use the Bold, Italic and Underline features to emphasize important data. This will improve the overall appearance of your worksheet.

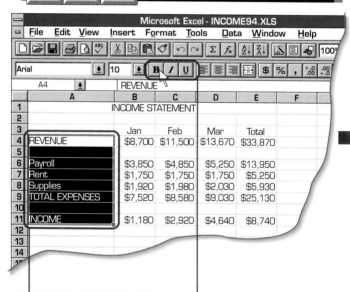

B **I** **U** BOLD, ITALIC AND UNDERLINE

1 Select the cells containing the data you want to change.

Note: To select cells, refer to pages 22 to 25.

2 Move the mouse ⬦ over one of the following options and then press the left button.

B Bold data

I Italicize data

U Underline data

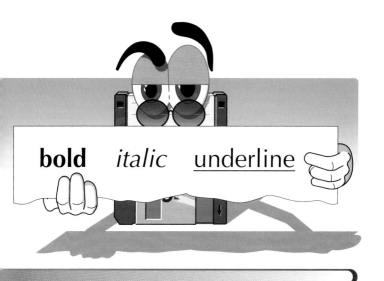

bold *italic* <u>underline</u>

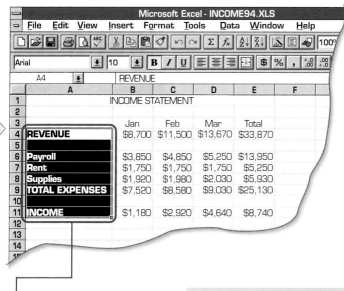

◆ The data in the cells you selected displays the new style.

Note: In this example, the data appears in the bold style.

REMOVE BOLD, ITALIC OR UNDERLINE

Repeat steps **1** and **2**.

CLEAR FORMATS

CLEAR FORMATS

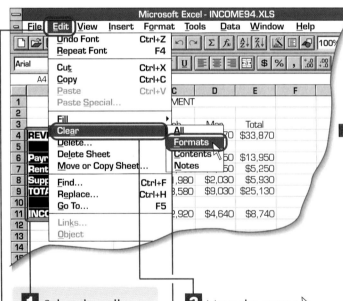

1 Select the cells displaying the formats you want to remove.

Note: To select cells, refer to pages 22 to 25.

2 Move the mouse ⌖ over **Edit** and then press the left button.

3 Move the mouse ⌖ over **Clear** and then press the left button.

4 Move the mouse ⌖ over **Formats** and then press the left button.

If you have applied several formats to cells in your worksheet, you can quickly remove all the formatting at once.

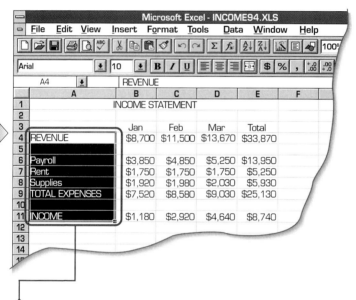

◆ All formats disappear from the cells you selected. The data remains unchanged.

CHANGE FONTS

CHANGE FONTS

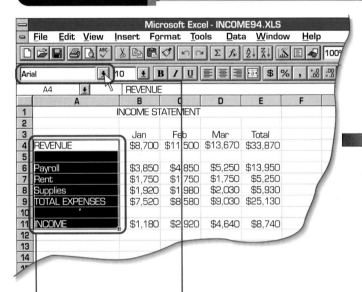

1 Select the cells containing the data you want to change to a new font.

Note: To select cells, refer to pages 22 to 25.

◆ The **Font** box displays the font of the active cell (example: **Arial**).

2 To display a list of the available fonts, move the mouse ⬚ over ⬆ beside the **Font** box and then press the left button.

You can change the design of data in your worksheet to emphasize headings.

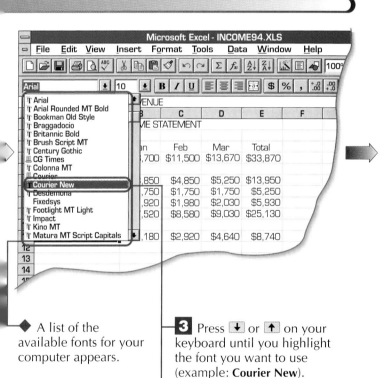

◆ A list of the available fonts for your computer appears.

3 Press ↓ or ↑ on your keyboard until you highlight the font you want to use (example: **Courier New**).

4 To select the highlighted font, press **Enter**.

To continue, refer to the next page.

CHANGE FONTS

You can change the size of data in your worksheet to make the data easier to read.

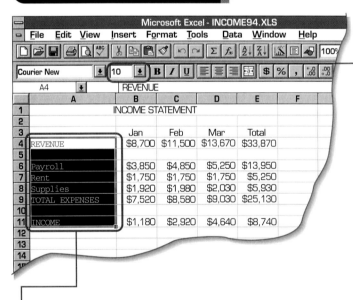

◆ The data in the cells you selected changes to the new font.

6 point

12 point

14 point

18 point

24 point

Excel measures the size of data in points. There are approximately 72 points per inch.

CHANGE FONT SIZE

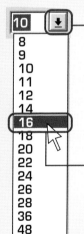

1 To change the size of data, select the cells containing the data you want to change.

Note: To select cells, refer to pages 22 to 25.

2 Move the mouse ⤢ over ⬇ beside the **Font Size:** box and then press the left button. A list of the available font sizes appears.

3 Move the mouse ⤢ over the font size you want to use (example: **16**) and then press the left button.

CHANGE FONTS

CHANGE FONTS

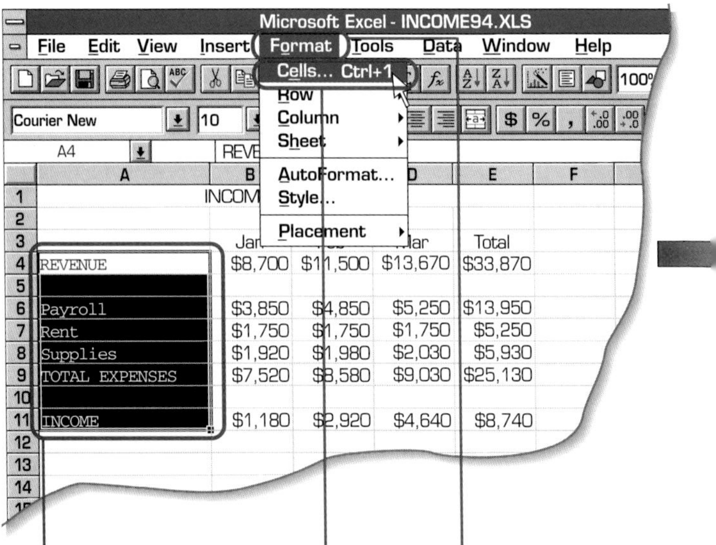

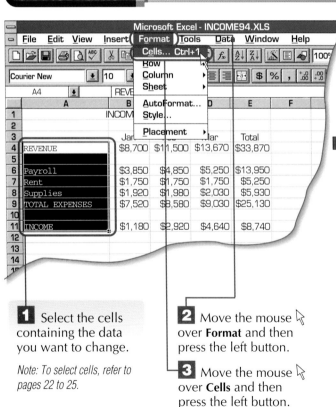

1 Select the cells containing the data you want to change.

Note: To select cells, refer to pages 22 to 25.

2 Move the mouse over **Format** and then press the left button.

3 Move the mouse over **Cells** and then press the left button.

You can change the design and size of data in your worksheet at the same time by using the Format Cells dialog box.

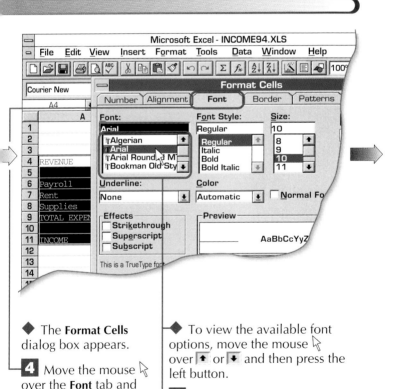

◆ The **Format Cells** dialog box appears.

4 Move the mouse ⬡ over the **Font** tab and then press the left button.

◆ To view the available font options, move the mouse ⬡ over ⬆ or ⬇ and then press the left button.

5 Move the mouse ⬡ over the font you want to use (example: **Arial**) and then press the left button.

To continue, refer to the next page.

157

CHANGE FONTS

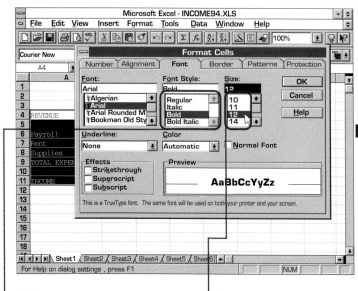

6 Move the mouse ⌖ over the font style you want to use (example: **Bold**) and then press the left button.

7 Move the mouse ⌖ over the font size you want to use (example: **12**) and then press the left button.

The Format Cells dialog box also lets you underline data in your worksheet.

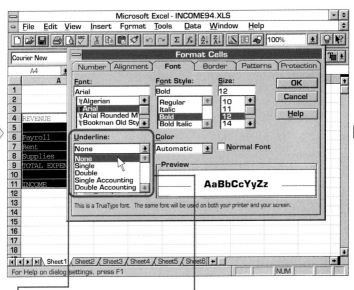

8 To select an underline style, move the mouse ⃗ over ⬇ in the **Underline:** box and then press the left button.

9 Move the mouse ⃗ over the underline style you want to use and then press the left button.

To continue, refer to the next page.

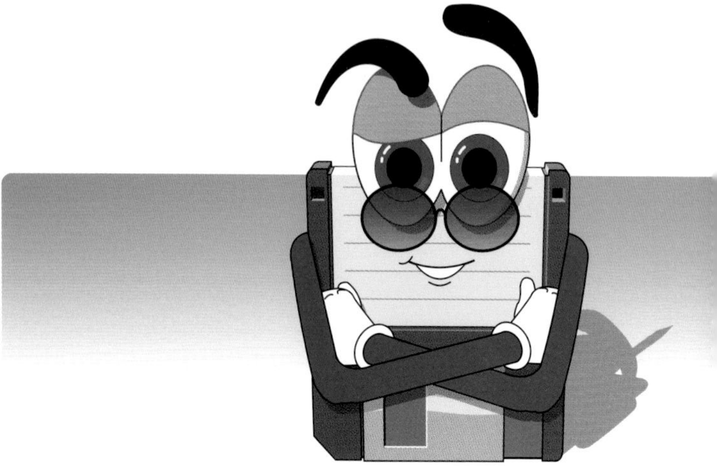

CHANGE FONTS (CONTINUED)

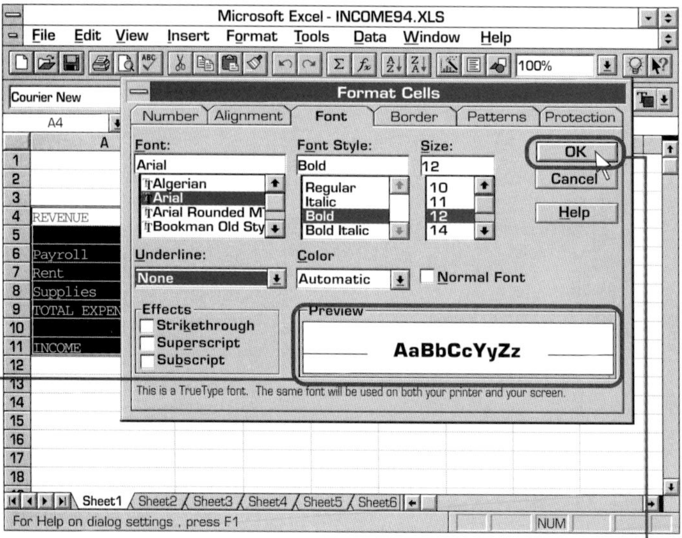

◆ This area displays a sample of the font options you selected.

10 To confirm the changes, move the mouse over **OK** and then press the left button.

The Format Cells
dialog box displays a
sample of the font options
you select. This lets you
see exactly how the data
will appear in your
worksheet.

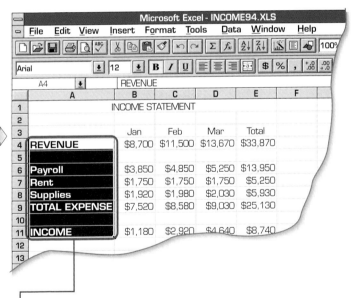

◆ The data in the cells
you selected displays the
font changes.

ADD BORDERS

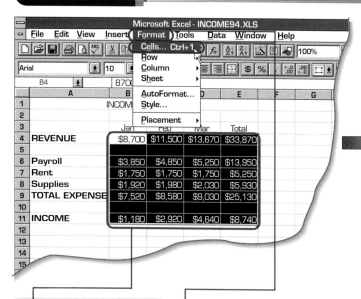

Microsoft Excel - INCOME94.XLS

File Edit View Insert **Format** Tools Data Window Help

Format menu:
- Cells... Ctrl+1
- Row
- Column
- Sheet
- AutoFormat...
- Style...
- Placement

Arial 10

B4 8700

	A	B		D	E	F	G
1		INCOM					
2							
3		Jan	Feb	Mar	Total		
4	**REVENUE**	$8,700	$11,500	$13,670	$33,870		
5							
6	Payroll	$3,850	$4,850	$5,250	$13,950		
7	Rent	$1,750	$1,750	$1,750	$5,250		
8	Supplies	$1,920	$1,980	$2,030	$5,930		
9	TOTAL EXPENSE	$7,520	$8,580	$9,030	$25,130		
10							
11	**INCOME**	$1,180	$2,920	$4,640	$8,740		
12							
13							
14							
15							

1 Select the cells you want to display borders.

Note: To select cells, refer to pages 22 to 25.

2 Move the mouse ⌖ over **Format** and then press the left button.

3 Move the mouse ⌖ over **Cells** and then press the left button.

162

You can add borders to draw attention to important data in your worksheet.

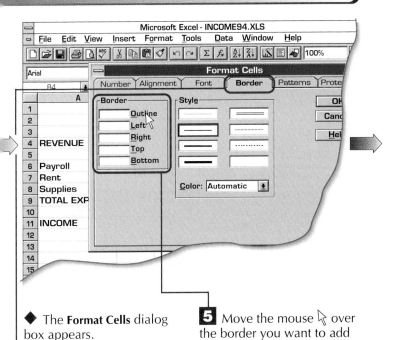

◆ The **Format Cells** dialog box appears.

4 Move the mouse ▷ over the **Border** tab and then press the left button.

5 Move the mouse ▷ over the border you want to add (example: **Outline**) and then press the left button.

To continue, refer to the next page.

163

ADD BORDERS

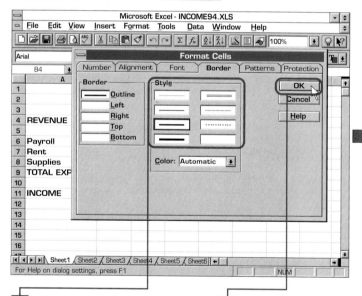

6 To select a line style for the border, move the mouse ⌖ over the style and then press the left button.

7 Repeat steps **5** and **6** for each border you want to add.

8 Move the mouse ⌖ over **OK** and then press the left button.

Excel offers several border styles that you can choose from.

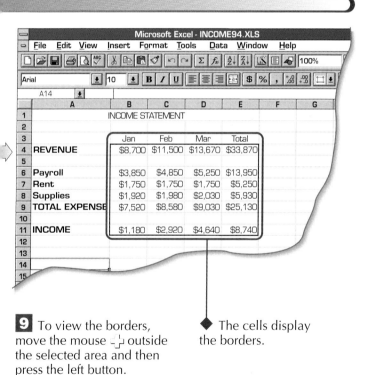

9 To view the borders, move the mouse ⌐┘ outside the selected area and then press the left button.

◆ The cells display the borders.

165

COPY FORMATS

If you like the appearance of a cell in your worksheet, you can copy the formats to other cells.

COPY FORMATS

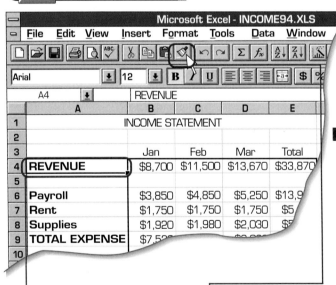

1 Move the mouse ⟳ over the cell displaying the formats you want to copy to other cells and then press the left button.

2 Move the mouse ⟱ over 🖌 and then press the left button (⟱ changes to ⟳🖌).

166

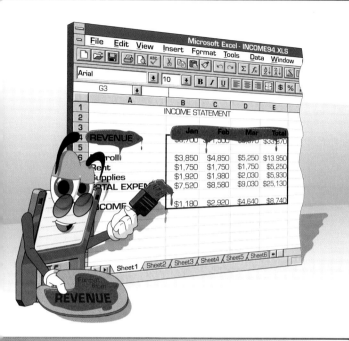

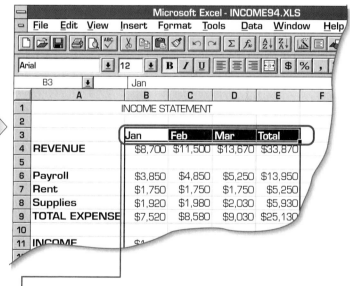

3 Select the cells you want to display the formats.

Note: To select cells, refer to pages 22 to 25.

◆ When you release the left button, the cells display the formats.

167

FORMAT A WORKSHEET AUTOMATICALLY

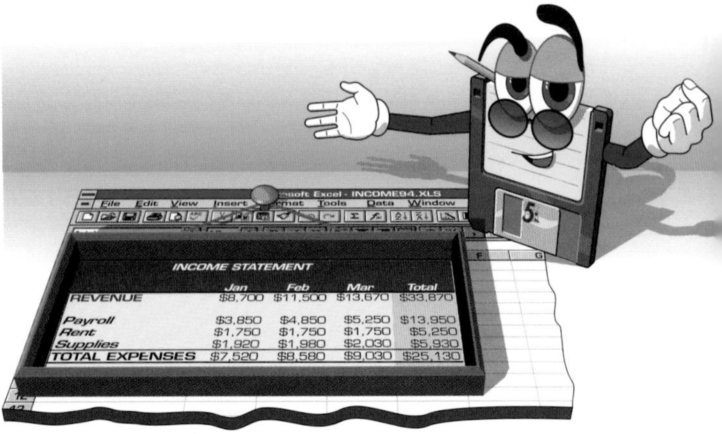

FORMAT A WORKSHEET AUTOMATICALLY

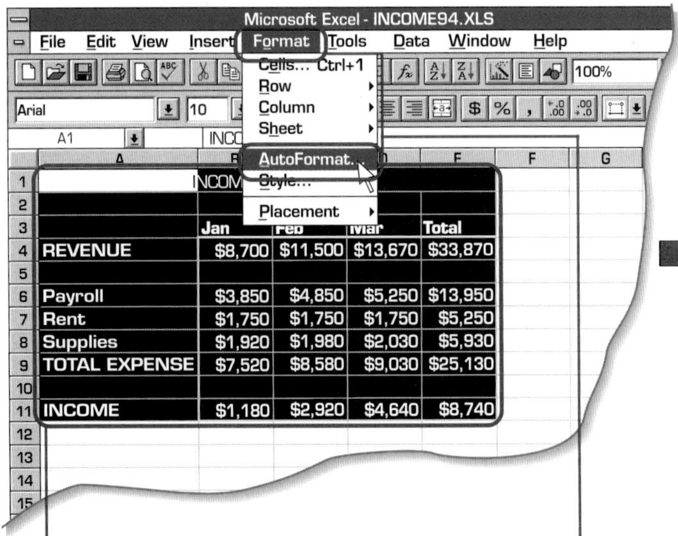

1 Select the cells you want to format.

Note: To select cells, refer to pages 22 to 25.

2 Move the mouse over **Format** and then press the left button.

3 Move the mouse over **AutoFormat** and then press the left button.

You can quickly format your worksheet by selecting one of many designs that Excel offers.

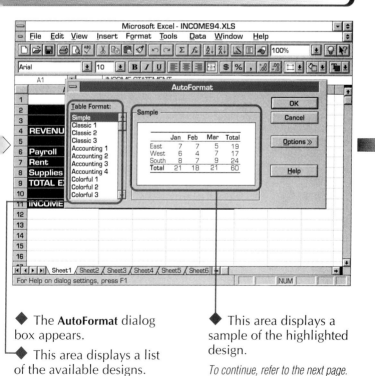

◆ The **AutoFormat** dialog box appears.

◆ This area displays a list of the available designs.

◆ This area displays a sample of the highlighted design.

To continue, refer to the next page.

169

FORMAT A WORKSHEET AUTOMATICALLY

The AutoFormat feature will enhance the appearance of your worksheet.

FORMAT A WORKSHEET (CONTINUED)

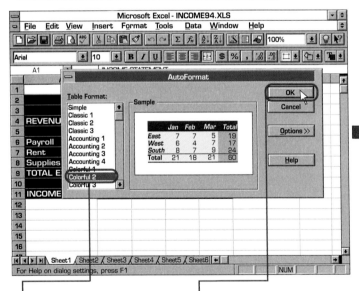

4 Press ↓ or ↑ on your keyboard until the **Sample** box displays the design you want to use (example: **Colorful 2**).

5 To select the highlighted design, move the mouse ↖ over **OK** and then press the left button.

REMOVE AN AUTOFORMAT DESIGN

1 Select the cells displaying the design you want to remove.

Note: To select cells, refer to pages 22 to 25.

2 Perform steps **2** to **5** starting on page 168, selecting **None** in step **4**.

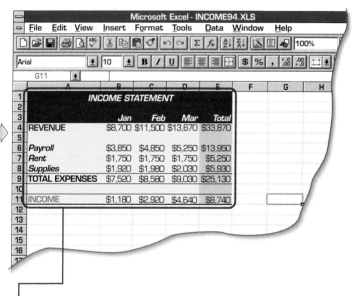

◆ Excel applies the design to the cells you selected.

Note: To deselect cells, move the mouse ⌐⌐ over any cell in your worksheet and then press the left button.

PREVIEW A WORKSHEET

 PREVIEW A WORKSHEET

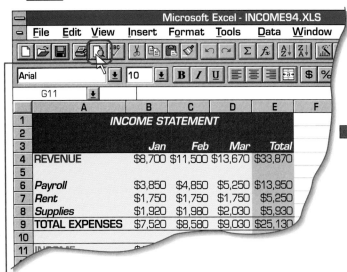

	Microsoft Excel - INCOME94.XLS					
File Edit View Insert Format Tools Data Window						

Arial | 10 | **B** *I* U | | | | $ %

G11

	A	B	C	D	E	F
1	*INCOME STATEMENT*					
2						
3		*Jan*	*Feb*	*Mar*	*Total*	
4	REVENUE	$8,700	$11,500	$13,670	$33,870	
5						
6	*Payroll*	$3,850	$4,850	$5,250	$13,950	
7	*Rent*	$1,750	$1,750	$1,750	$5,250	
8	*Supplies*	$1,920	$1,980	$2,030	$5,930	
9	TOTAL EXPENSES	$7,520	$8,580	$9,030	$25,130	
10						
11						

1 To display your worksheet in the Print Preview window, move the mouse ⇦ over [🔍] and then press the left button.

The Print Preview feature lets you see on screen what your worksheet will look like when printed.

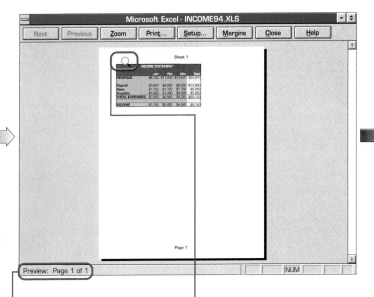

◆ The first page of your worksheet appears.

◆ The status bar at the bottom of your screen tells you which page you are viewing.

2 To magnify an area of the page, move the mouse ⅄ over the area (⅄ changes to ◯) and then press the left button.

To continue, refer to the next page.

173

PREVIEW A WORKSHEET

If your worksheet consists of more than one page, you can use the Next and Previous buttons to switch between the pages in the Print Preview window.

PREVIEW A WORKSHEET (CONTINUED)

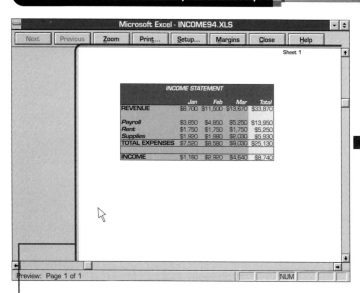

◆ A magnified view of the area appears.

◆ To browse through the page, press ⬇, ⬆, ➡ or ⬅ on your keyboard.

3 To again display the entire page, move the mouse ⬉ anywhere over the page and then press the left button.

174

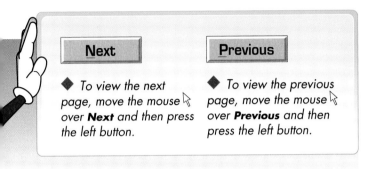

Next	Previous
◆ To view the next page, move the mouse over **Next** and then press the left button.	◆ To view the previous page, move the mouse over **Previous** and then press the left button.

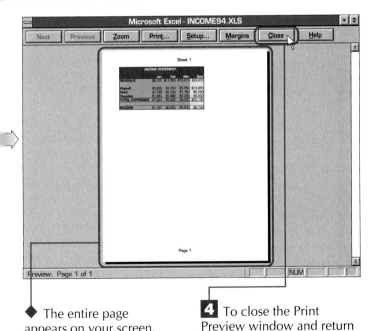

◆ The entire page appears on your screen.

4 To close the Print Preview window and return to your worksheet, move the mouse over **Close** and then press the left button.

CHANGE MARGINS

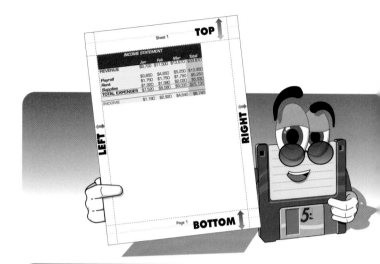

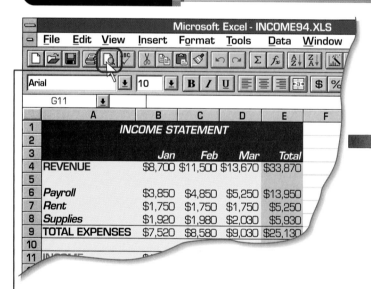

1 To display your worksheet in the Print Preview window, move the mouse ↖ over 🔍 and then press the left button.

A margin is the amount of space between data and the edges of your paper. You can change the margins for your worksheet in the Print Preview window.

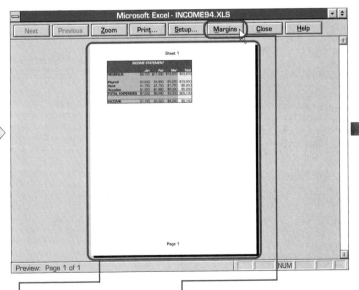

◆ The first page of your worksheet appears.

Note: For more information on using the Print Preview feature, refer to page 172.

2 To display the margins, move the mouse ⌖ over **Margins** and then press the left button.

◆ To hide the margins, repeat step **2**.

To continue, refer to the next page.

CHANGE MARGINS

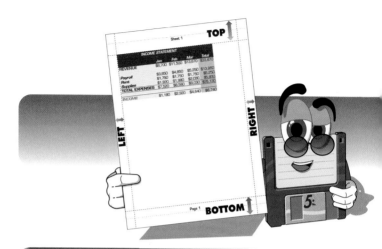

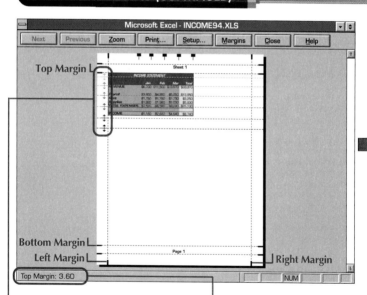

3 To change the position of a margin, move the mouse ⌖ over the margin handle and ⌖ changes to ‡ or ↔.

4 Press and hold down the left button as you drag the margin to a new location.

◆ A dotted line indicates the location of the new margin.

◆ The bottom of your screen displays the new measurement as you drag the margin.

178

When you begin a worksheet, the top and bottom margins are set at 1 inch. The left and right margins are set at 0.75 inches.

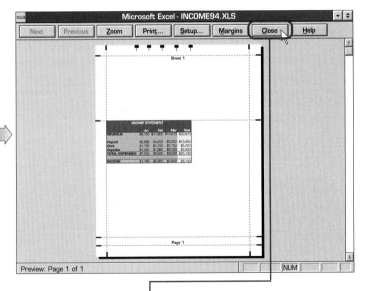

5 Release the button to display the new margin.

6 To close the Print Preview window and return to your worksheet, move the mouse ⌖ over **Close** and then press the left button.

Note: Margins are only visible when you display your worksheet in the Print Preview window.

PRINT A WORKSHEET

> You can print your entire worksheet or a section of data.

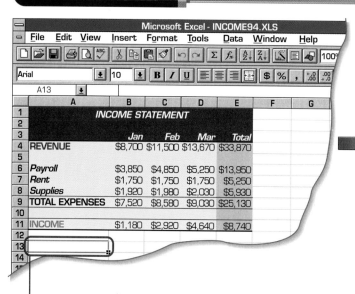

1 To print your entire worksheet, move the mouse ⊕ over any cell in the worksheet and then press the left button.

◆ To print a section of your worksheet, select the cells you want to print.

Note: To select cells, refer to pages 22 to 25.

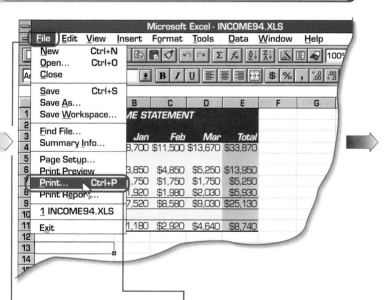

2 Move the mouse ↖ over **File** and then press the left button.

3 Move the mouse ↖ over **Print** and then press the left button.

◆ The **Print** dialog box appears.

To continue, refer to the next page.

PRINT A WORKSHEET

Before printing, make sure your printer is on and it contains paper.

PRINT A WORKSHEET (CONTINUED)

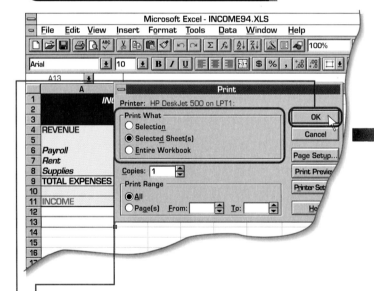

4 Move the mouse ⬐ over the print option you want to use and then press the left button (○ changes to ◉).

5 Move the mouse ⬐ over **OK** and then press the left button.

PRINT OPTIONS

Selection
Prints the data you selected.

Selected Sheet(s)
Prints your entire worksheet.

Entire Workbook
Prints all the worksheets in your workbook.

◆ To quickly print your entire worksheet, move the mouse ⟲ over 🖨 and then press the left button.

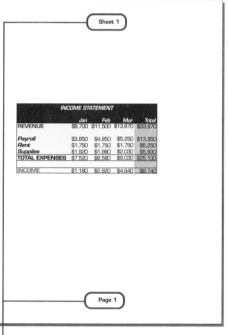

A colored worksheet printed on a black and white printer can be difficult to read. To print your worksheet in black and white, refer to page 184.

◆ The worksheet name and page number appear on every page you print. To change a header or footer, refer to page 188.

CHANGE PRINT OPTIONS

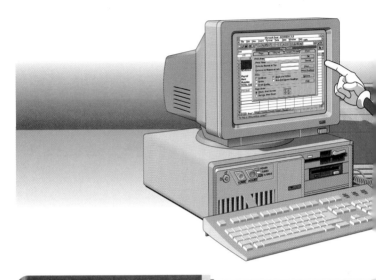

CHANGE PRINT OPTIONS

◆ **Gridlines -** prints lines that separate the cells in your worksheet.

◆ **Row and Column Headings -** prints the row and column headings as they appear on screen.

◆ **Black and White -** prints your worksheet in black and white. A colored worksheet printed on a black and white printer may be difficult to read. Use this option to avoid problems.

◆ **Draft Quality -** prints fewer graphics and does not print gridlines. This reduces printing time.

You can use the Page Setup dialog box to change the way your worksheet appears on a printed page.

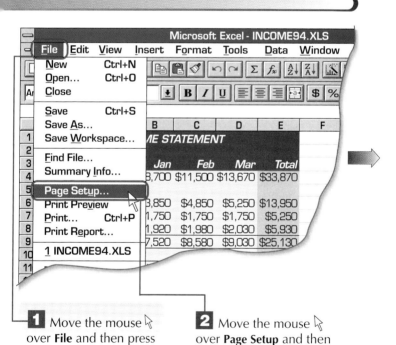

1 Move the mouse ⌕ over **File** and then press the left button.

2 Move the mouse ⌕ over **Page Setup** and then press the left button.

To continue, refer to the next page.

185

CHANGE PRINT OPTIONS

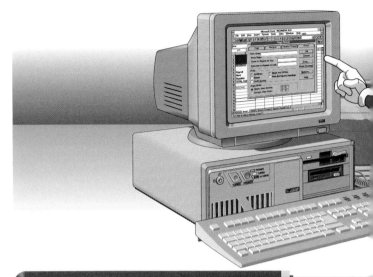

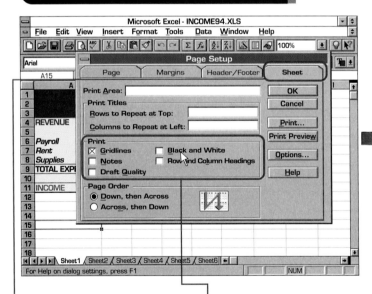

◆ The **Page Setup** dialog box appears.

3 Move the mouse ⬦ over the **Sheet** tab and then press the left button.

4 Move the mouse ⬦ over an option you want to use (example: **Black and White**) and then press the left button.

Note: ⊠ indicates an option is on.
☐ indicates an option is off.

The options you select in the Page Setup dialog box will not change how the worksheet appears on your screen.

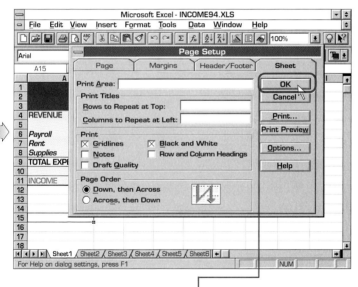

5 Repeat step **4** for each option you want to use.

6 To confirm the change(s), move the mouse ⌖ over **OK** and then press the left button.

ADD A HEADER OR FOOTER

Headers and footers print information at the top and bottom of each page.

ADD A HEADER OR FOOTER

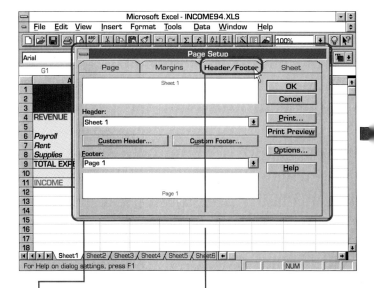

1 To add a header or footer, display the **Page Setup** dialog box.

*Note: To display the **Page Setup** dialog box, perform steps **1** and **2** on page 185.*

2 Move the mouse ⬡ over the **Header/Footer** tab and then press the left button.

Header

Excel automatically prints the name of the worksheet at the top of each page. You can change this header at any time.

Footer

Excel automatically prints the page number at the bottom of each page. You can change this footer at any time.

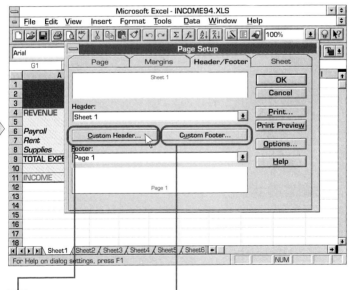

3 To create a header, move the mouse � over **Custom Header** and then press the left button.

◆ To create a footer, move the mouse � over **Custom Footer** and then press the left button.

To continue, refer to the next page.

ADD A HEADER OR FOOTER

> Headers and footers may include the title of your worksheet, the date or your company name.

ADD A HEADER OR FOOTER (CONTINUED)

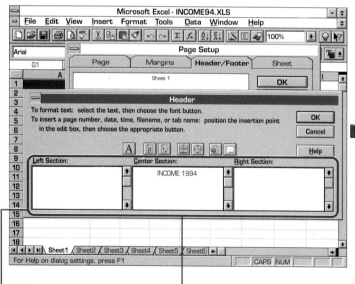

4 Move the mouse ↕ over the box under **Center Section:** and then press the left button.

5 To remove the existing text, press `Delete` or `←Backspace` until the text disappears.

6 Move the mouse ↕ over the box for the area of the page where you want to display the header or footer and then press the left button.

7 Type the text (example: **INCOME 1994**).

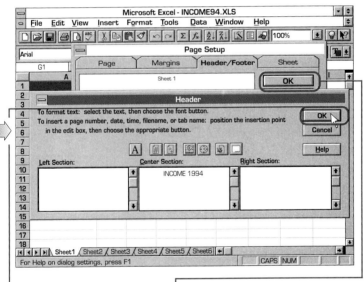

8 Move the mouse ⓚ over **OK** and then press the left button.

9 Move the mouse ⓚ over **OK** in the **Page Setup** dialog box and then press the left button.

*Note: Headers and footers are only visible when you display your worksheet in the **Print Preview** window. For more information, refer to page 172.*

191

ZOOM IN OR OUT

ZOOM TO A SPECIFIC PERCENTAGE

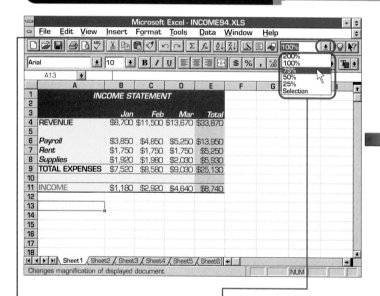

When you first start Excel, your worksheet appears in the 100% zoom setting.

1 To display your worksheet using a different setting, move the mouse ☐ over ☐ beside the **Zoom Control** box and then press the left button.

◆ A list of zoom settings appears.

2 Move the mouse ☐ over the zoom setting you want to use (example: **75%**) and then press the left button.

You can magnify a worksheet to read small data or shrink a worksheet to view more of your data.

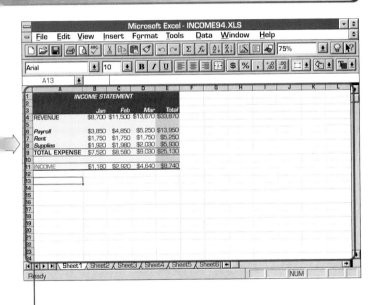

◆ Your worksheet appears in the new zoom setting.

Note: When you change the zoom setting, the changes will not affect the way the data appears on a printed page.

DISPLAY OR HIDE TOOLBARS

Excel offers thirteen different toolbars that you can display or hide at any time. Each toolbar contains a series of buttons that let you quickly select commands.

DISPLAY OR HIDE TOOLBARS

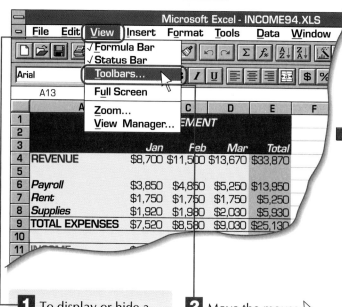

1 To display or hide a toolbar, move the mouse ᰔ over **View** and then press the left button.

2 Move the mouse ᰔ over **Toolbars** and then press the left button.

194

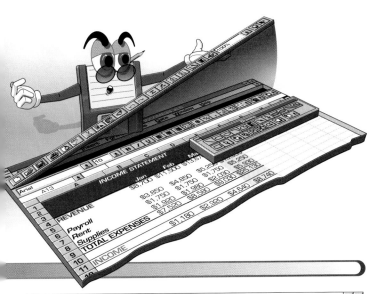

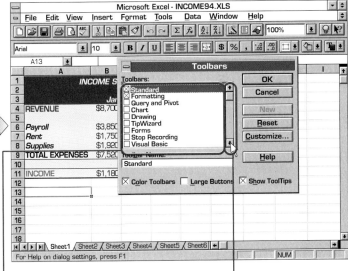

◆ The **Toolbars** dialog box appears.

◆ This area displays a list of the available toolbars.

3 To view more toolbar names, move the mouse ⌖ over ⬇ or ⬆ and then press the left button.

To continue, refer to the next page.

195

DISPLAY OR HIDE TOOLBARS

A screen displaying fewer toolbars provides a larger and less cluttered working area.

DISPLAY OR HIDE TOOLBARS (CONTINUED)

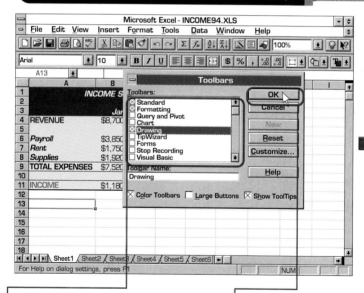

4 To display a toolbar, move the mouse ⌖ over the toolbar name and then press the left button (☐ changes to ☒).

◆ To hide a toolbar, move the mouse ⌖ over the toolbar name and then press the left button (☒ changes to ☐).

5 Move the mouse ⌖ over **OK** and then press the left button.

196

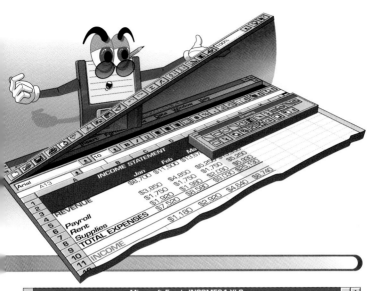

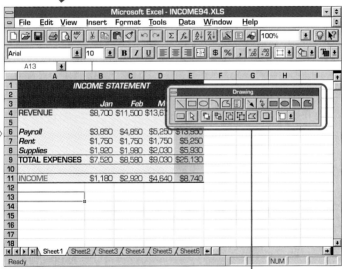

◆ Excel displays or hides
the toolbar(s) you selected.

197

SWITCH BETWEEN WORKSHEETS

SWITCH BETWEEN WORKSHEETS

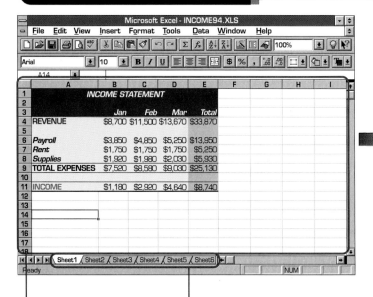

◆ The worksheet displayed on your screen is one of 16 worksheets in the current workbook.

◆ The current worksheet displays a white tab.

◆ The other worksheets display gray tabs.

The worksheet displayed on your screen is part of a workbook. Like a three-ring binder, a workbook contains several sheets that you can easily flip through. This lets you view the contents of each worksheet.

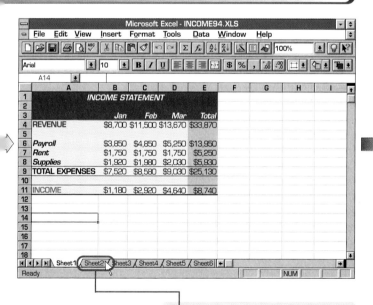

◆ The contents of the current worksheet are displayed on your screen. The contents of the other worksheets are hidden behind this worksheet.

1 To display the contents of another worksheet, move the mouse ⬚ over the worksheet tab (example: **Sheet2**) and then press the left button.

To continue, refer to the next page.

199

SWITCH BETWEEN WORKSHEETS

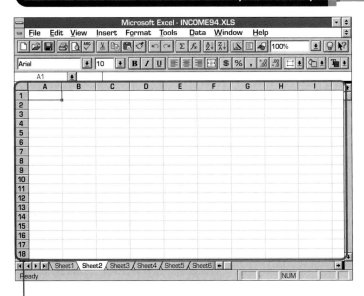

◆ The contents of the
worksheet appear.

You can use the worksheets in a workbook to store related information. For example, you can store information for each division of a company on separate worksheets.

Excel cannot fit the names of all the worksheets at the bottom of your screen. You can use these arrows to display the other worksheet tabs.

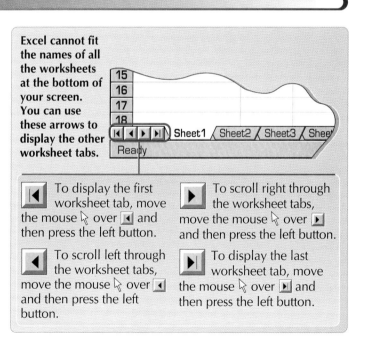

To display the first worksheet tab, move the mouse ⬚ over ◄ and then press the left button.

To scroll right through the worksheet tabs, move the mouse ⬚ over ► and then press the left button.

To scroll left through the worksheet tabs, move the mouse ⬚ over ◄ and then press the left button.

To display the last worksheet tab, move the mouse ⬚ over ► and then press the left button.

COPY OR MOVE DATA BETWEEN WORKSHEETS

Copying or moving data between worksheets saves you time when you are working in one worksheet and want to use data from another.

COPY OR MOVE DATA BETWEEN WORKSHEETS

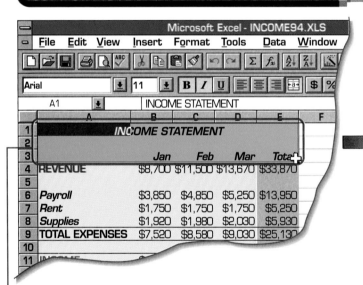

1 Select the cells containing the data you want to copy or move to another worksheet.

Note: To select cells, refer to pages 22 to 25.

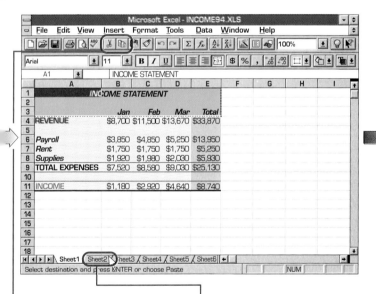

2 To copy the data, move the mouse ↖ over 🗐 and then press the left button.

◆ To move the data, move the mouse ↖ over ✂ and then press the left button.

3 Move the mouse ↖ over the tab of the worksheet where you want to place the data and then press the left button.

To continue, refer to the next page.

COPY OR MOVE DATA BETWEEN WORKSHEETS

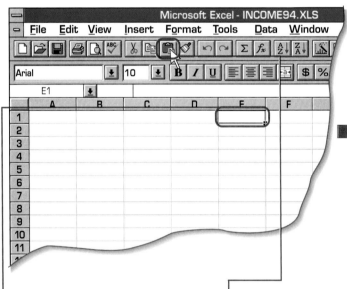

◆ The worksheet appears on your screen.

4 Move the mouse ⊕ over the cell where you want to place the data and then press the left button. This cell will become the top left cell of the new location.

5 Move the mouse ⍏ over 📋 and then press the left button.

COPY DATA

When you copy data, Excel copies the data and pastes the copy in a new location. The original data remains in its place.

MOVE DATA

When you move data, Excel cuts the data and pastes it in a new location. The original data disappears.

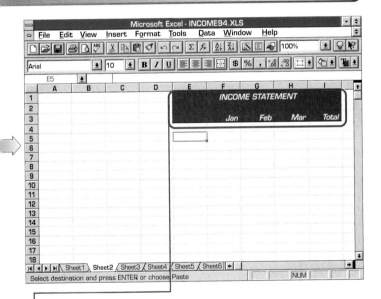

◆ The data appears in the new location.

◆ To deselect cells, move the mouse -⌐ over any cell in your worksheet and then press the left button.

CREATE A NEW WORKBOOK

You can create a new workbook to store data on a different topic.

CREATE A NEW WORKBOOK

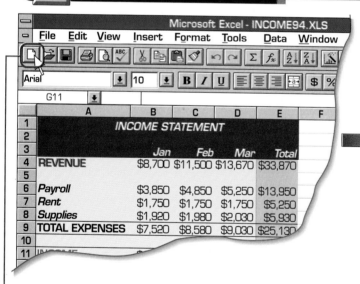

Microsoft Excel - INCOME94.XLS

File   Edit   View   Insert   Format   Tools   Data   Window

Arial   10   B I U │ ═ ═ ═ ═ │ $ %

G11

	A	B	C	D	E	F
1	INCOME STATEMENT					
2						
3		Jan	Feb	Mar	Total	
4	REVENUE	$8,700	$11,500	$13,670	$33,870	
5						
6	Payroll	$3,850	$4,850	$5,250	$13,950	
7	Rent	$1,750	$1,750	$1,750	$5,250	
8	Supplies	$1,920	$1,980	$2,030	$5,930	
9	TOTAL EXPENSES	$7,520	$8,580	$9,030	$25,130	
10						
11	INCOME					

1 To create a new workbook, move the mouse ⌖ over 🗋 and then press the left button.

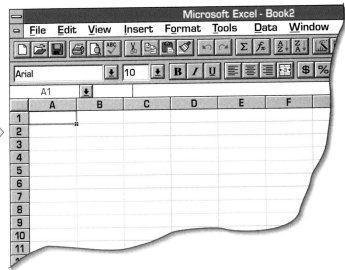

◆ A new workbook appears.

Note: The previous workbook is now hidden behind the new workbook.

SWITCH BETWEEN WORKBOOKS

You can easily switch between all of your open workbooks.

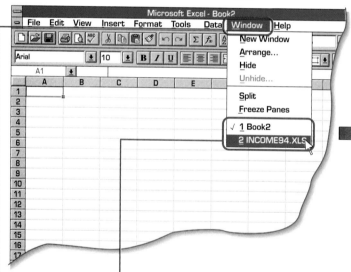

Microsoft Excel - Book2

File   Edit   View   Insert   Format   Tools   Data   **Window**   Help

New Window
Arrange...
Hide
Unhide...

Split
Freeze Panes

√ 1 Book2
2 INCOME94.XLS

1 Move the mouse ⇖ over **Window** and then press the left button.

◆ A list of all your open workbooks appears. The current workbook displays a check mark (√) beside its name.

2 Move the mouse ⇖ over the workbook you want to switch to (example: **INCOME94.XLS**) and then press the left button.

208

◆ The workbook appears.

◆ Excel displays the name of the workbook at the top of your screen.

CLOSE A WORKBOOK

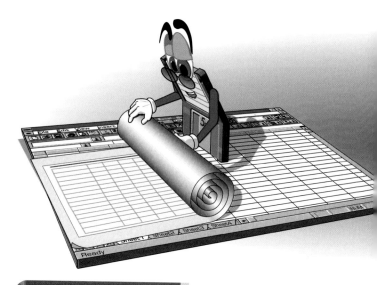

CLOSE A WORKBOOK

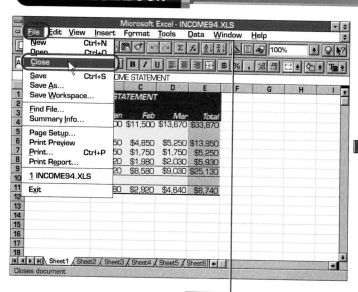

1 To save the workbook before closing, refer to page 50.

2 Move the mouse ⩗ over **File** and then press the left button.

3 Move the mouse ⩗ over **Close** and then press the left button.

When you finish working with a workbook, you can close it to remove the workbook from your screen.

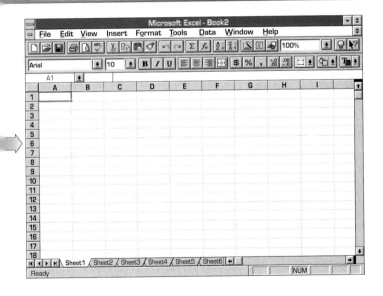

◆ The workbook disappears from your screen.

◆ If you had more than one workbook open, the second last workbook you worked on appears.

211

INTRODUCTION

You can create a chart to visually display your worksheet data.

PARTS OF A CHART

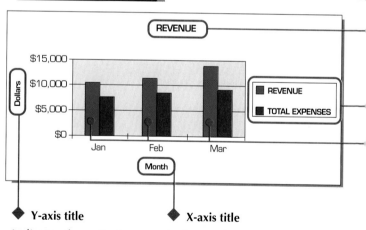

◆ **Y-axis title**

Indicates the unit of measure used in the chart (example: **Dollars**).

◆ **X-axis title**

Indicates the categories used in the chart (example: **Month**).

◆ **Chart title**

Identifies the chart.

◆ **Legend**

Defines the symbols used for each data series in the chart (example: ■ represents **REVENUE**).

◆ **Data series**

A group of related data representing a row or column from the worksheet (example: **Revenue**). A chart consists of one or more data series.

CHART TYPES

AREA

Each line represents a data series. The area below each line is filled in. This is useful for showing the amount of change in values over time (example: sales figures for the last five years).

BAR

Each horizontal bar represents a value in a data series. This chart shows differences between values (example: a comparison of revenue and expenses for each month in a year).

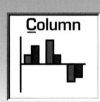

COLUMN

This chart is similar to a bar chart, except vertical bars represent the values in a data series.

LINE

Each line represents a data series. This is useful for showing the rate of change in values over time.

PIE

This chart shows each value in a data series as a piece of a pie. A pie chart can only display one data series at a time. This is useful for showing percentages (example: January sales as a percentage of sales for the year).

DOUGHNUT

This chart is similar to a pie chart except it can display more than one data series at a time. Each ring represents a data series.

RADAR

This chart represents each data series as a line around a central point (example: each month is an axis, the distance from the center point shows the sales for the month).

XY (SCATTER)

This chart shows the relationship between two or more data series (example: relationship between education and life-time earnings).

CREATE A CHART

You can use the ChartWizard to create a chart directly from your worksheet data.

STEP 1 — SELECT DATA FOR THE CHART

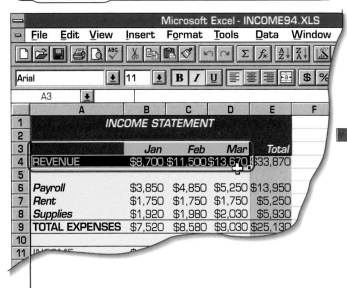

	A	B	C	D	E	F
1	INCOME STATEMENT					
2						
3		Jan	Feb	Mar	Total	
4	REVENUE	$8,700	$11,500	$13,670	$33,870	
5						
6	Payroll	$3,850	$4,850	$5,250	$13,950	
7	Rent	$1,750	$1,750	$1,750	$5,250	
8	Supplies	$1,920	$1,980	$2,030	$5,930	
9	TOTAL EXPENSES	$7,520	$8,580	$9,030	$25,130	
10						
11						

1 Select the cells containing the data you want to chart, including the row and column headings.

Note: To select cells, refer to pages 22 to 25.

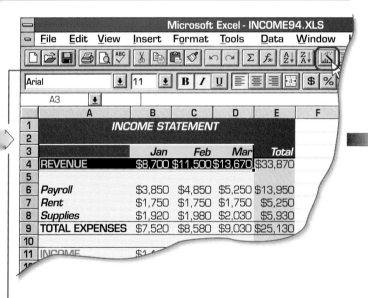

2 Move the mouse ⌖ over 📊 and then press the left button (⌖ changes to ⁺₍ₗₗ₎).

To continue, refer to the next page.

CREATE A CHART

The ChartWizard leads you through each step of creating a chart.

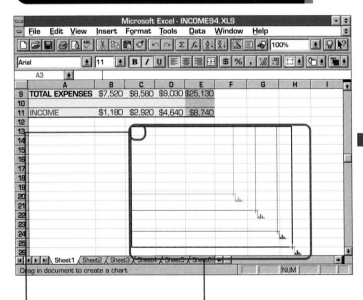

3 Move the mouse +.ıl. over the location where you want the top left corner of the chart to appear.

4 Press and hold down the left button as you drag the mouse +.ıl. until the rectangle displays the size of the chart you want. Then release the button.

218

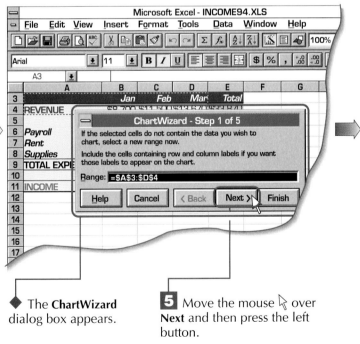

◆ The **ChartWizard** dialog box appears.

5 Move the mouse ▷ over **Next** and then press the left button.

To continue, refer to the next page.

CREATE A CHART

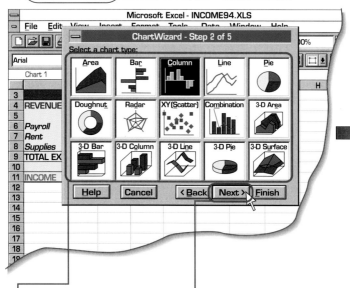

6 To select a chart type, move the mouse ⬀ over the type you want to use (example: **Column**) and then press the left button.

7 To display the next step, move the mouse ⬀ over **Next** and then press the left button.

220

You can cancel the creation of a chart at any time by using the Cancel button.

◆ To cancel the creation of a chart, move the mouse ↖ over **Cancel** and then press the left button.

STEP 3 SELECT A CHART FORMAT

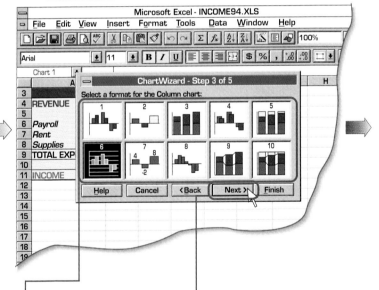

8 To select a format for the chart type you selected, move the mouse ↖ over the format you want to use (example: **6**) and then press the left button.

9 To display the next step, move the mouse ↖ over **Next** and then press the left button.

To continue, refer to the next page.

CREATE A CHART

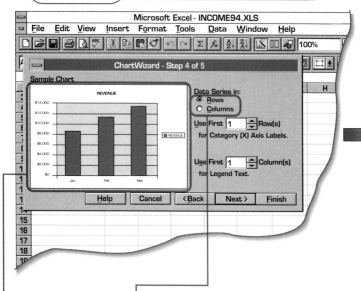

◆ This area displays a sample of your chart.

Note: The options in this dialog box depend on the chart type you selected in step 6.

10 To make each data series represent a row of data from your worksheet, move the mouse ⌖ over **Rows** and then press the left button.

◆ To make each data series represent a column of data from your worksheet, move the mouse ⌖ over **Columns** and then press the left button.

222

You can
return to a previous
step at any time
by using the
Back button.

◆ To return to the previous
step, move the mouse ⌖ over
Back and then press the left
button.

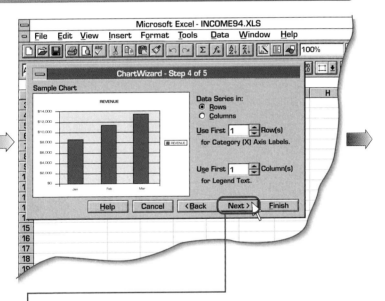

11 To display the next step,
move the mouse ⌖ over **Next**
and then press the left button.

*To continue, refer to
the next page.*

CREATE A CHART

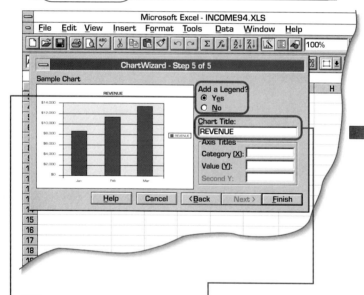

12 To create a chart with a legend, move the mouse ↖ over **Yes** and then press the left button.

◆ To create a chart without a legend, move the mouse ↖ over **No** and then press the left button.

13 To add a title to the chart, press **Tab** and then type the title (example: **REVENUE**).

You can add a legend and titles to your chart to make your data more meaningful.

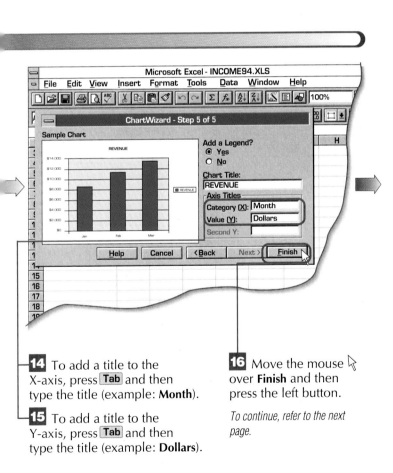

14 To add a title to the X-axis, press **Tab** and then type the title (example: **Month**).

15 To add a title to the Y-axis, press **Tab** and then type the title (example: **Dollars**).

16 Move the mouse ⌖ over **Finish** and then press the left button.

To continue, refer to the next page.

CREATE A CHART

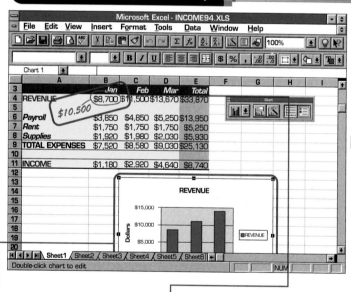

◆ The chart appears.

◆ If you make changes to the data in your worksheet, Excel automatically updates the chart to reflect the changes.

*Note: In this example, the data in **B4** changes from **$8,700** to **$10,500**.*

To save
a chart, you
must save the
workbook.

Note: For information on saving
a workbook, refer to page 50.

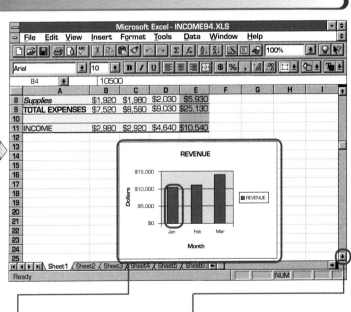

◆ The changes made to
the data in your worksheet
appear in the chart.

◆ To view your entire chart,
move the mouse ⃗ over ⬇
and then press the left button.

MOVE A CHART

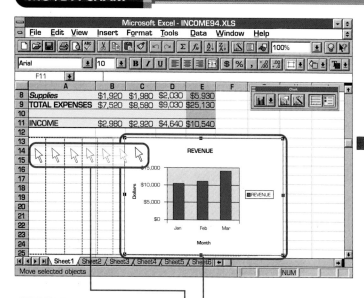

1 To deselect a chart, move the mouse ✛ over any cell outside the chart and then press the left button.

2 To move a chart, move the mouse ⇦ anywhere over the chart.

3 Press and hold down the left button as you drag the chart to a new location.

◆ A dotted rectangular box shows the new location.

228

After you create
a chart, you can move it
to a more suitable
location in your
worksheet.

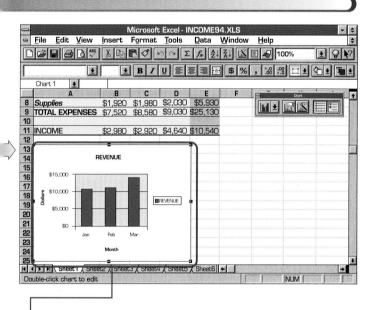

4 Release the button and
the chart moves to the new
location.

SIZE A CHART

You can change the size of a chart using any handle around the chart.

SIZE A CHART

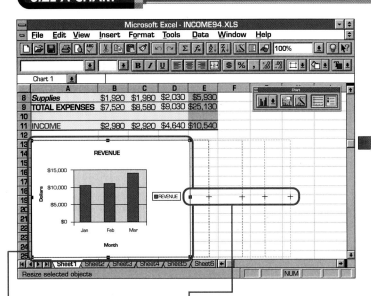

1 To deselect a chart, move the mouse ⇦ over any cell outside the chart and then press the left button.

2 Move the mouse ▷ anywhere over the chart and then press the left button. Handles (■) appear around the chart.

3 Move the mouse ▷ over one of the handles (■) and ▷ changes to ↔.

4 Press and hold down the left button as you drag the chart to the new size.

◆ A dotted rectangular box shows the new size.

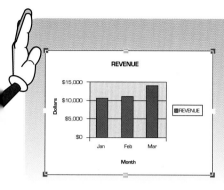

■ These handles change the height of a chart.

□ These handles change the width of a chart.

■ These handles change the height and width of a chart at the same time.

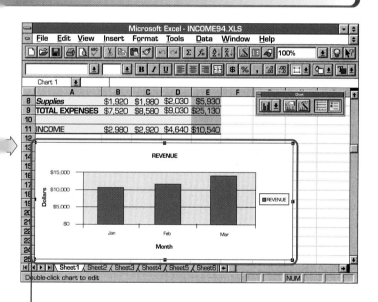

5 Release the button and the chart displays the new size.

PRINT A CHART

> You can print your chart with the worksheet data.

PRINT A CHART WITH WORKSHEET DATA

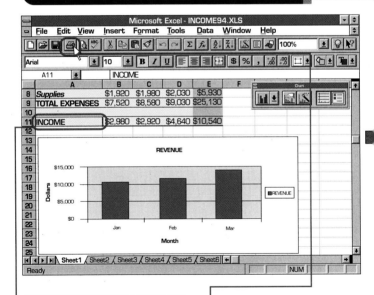

1 Move the mouse ⊕ over any cell outside the chart and then press the left button.

2 Move the mouse ⌖ over 🖨 and then press the left button.

Note: For more information on printing, refer to page 180.

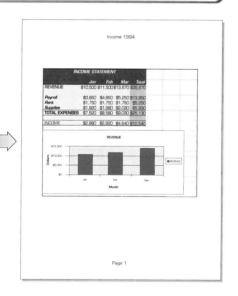

Note: A colorful chart can be difficult to read when printed on a black and white printer. To avoid problems, print the chart in black and white. For more information, refer to page 184.

PRINT A CHART

> You can print your chart on its own page, without the worksheet data.

PRINT A CHART ON ITS OWN PAGE

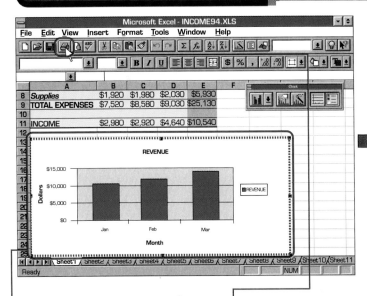

◆ To print a chart on its own page, you must first select the chart. A selected chart displays a colored border.

1 To select a chart, move the mouse ⍺ anywhere over the chart then quickly press the left button twice.

2 Move the mouse ⍺ over 🖨 and then press the left button.

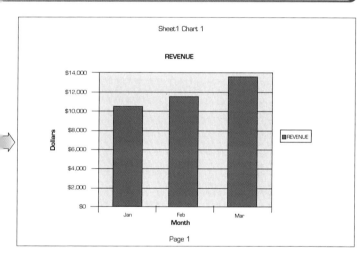

CHANGE CHART TYPE

After creating a chart, you can select a new type that will better suit your data.

CHANGE CHART TYPE

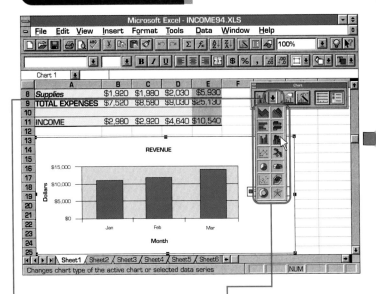

1 Move the mouse ⊵ anywhere over the chart and then press the left button.

2 Move the mouse ⊵ over ⬇ on the **Chart** toolbar and then press the left button.

*Note: To display the **Chart** toolbar, refer to page 194.*

◆ The available chart types appear.

3 Move the mouse ⊵ over the chart type you want to use and then press the left button.

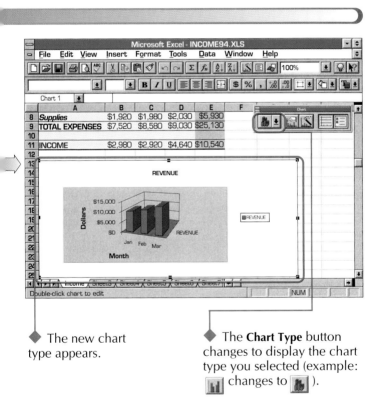

◆ The new chart type appears.

◆ The **Chart Type** button changes to display the chart type you selected (example: ⬚ changes to ⬚).

FORMAT A CHART AUTOMATICALLY

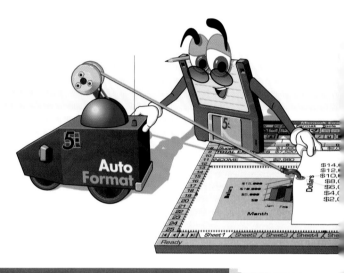

FORMAT A CHART AUTOMATICALLY

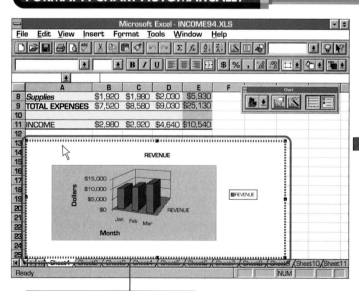

◆ You must first select the chart you want to format. A selected chart displays a colored border.

1 To select a chart, move the mouse ⯈ anywhere over the chart and then quickly press the left button twice.

238

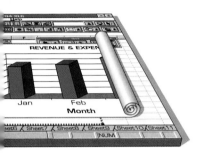

The AutoFormat feature provides a selection of formats that you can choose from to enhance the appearance of your chart.

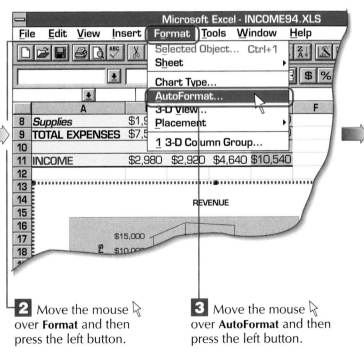

2 Move the mouse ⃗ over **Format** and then press the left button.

3 Move the mouse ⃗ over **AutoFormat** and then press the left button.

To continue, refer to the next page.

239

FORMAT A CHART AUTOMATICALLY

FORMAT A CHART (CONTINUED)

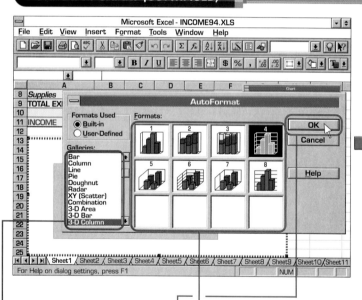

◆ The **AutoFormat** dialog box appears.

4 Move the mouse ⟍ over the chart type you want to use (example: **3-D Column**) and then press the left button.

5 Move the mouse ⟍ over the format you want to use (example: **4**) and then press the left button.

6 Move the mouse ⟍ over **OK** and then press the left button.

240

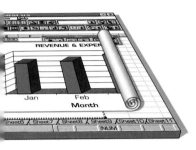

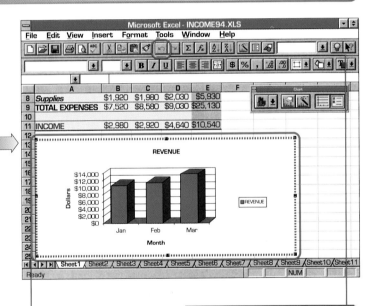

◆ Your chart displays the new format.

REMOVE AUTOFORMAT

To undo the AutoFormat immediately after applying the format, move the mouse ▷ over ▣ and then press the left button.

241

INDEX

INDEX